Dealing
WITH A
SOCIOPATH

Dealing
— WITH A —
SOCIOPATH

How to survive the antisocials, narcissists and psychopaths in your life

DONNA ANDERSEN

Anderly Publishing
Egg Harbor Township, New Jersey

Back cover photography by Bill Horin

Anderly Publishing
3121-D Fire Road, #304
Egg Harbor Township, NJ 08234 USA
www.anderlypublishing.com

Library of Congress Control Number: 2019957654
ISBN: 978-1-951347-04-8

First softcover edition January 2020

Contents

Introduction

Sociopaths are profoundly different from the rest of us. If you have to interact with sociopaths, you must keep this in mind, and adjust your approach accordingly.

You cannot blindly accept their words as truth.

You cannot trust them to do what is right.

You need to figure out their ulterior motives.

I learned all this the hard way. Back in 1996, I met and married a man, James Alwyn Montgomery, who turned out to be a sociopath. At the time, I had no idea that someone who dressed well, spoke well and proclaimed that he was head-over-heels in love with me could be a fraud and a con artist.

During our short, two-year marriage, Montgomery took $227,000 from me, left me in debt, cheated with multiple women, had a child with one of those women, and then, after I left him but before we divorced, committed bigamy by marrying her.

When I finally sorted through the treasure trove of papers that he left in my basement, which, respecting his privacy I previously ignored, I discovered that I was not his only victim. James Montgomery lived his life by swindling money from women.

Because of my experience, I founded Lovefraud.com in 2005. Since then, I've learned that the problem of sociopaths is even more widespread than I ever dreamed, and they exploit people for more than money.

What's a sociopath?

Let's clarify whom we are talking about. On Lovefraud.com, I use the word "sociopath" as an umbrella term to describe people who have serious personality disorders in which they manipulate and exploit others. Clinically, they would be diagnosed as having antisocial, narcissistic, borderline, histrionic or psychopathic personality disorders.

Today, the word "sociopath" is not an official diagnosis at all. Instead, psychiatrists and therapists use "sociopath" as shorthand for "antisocial personality disorder." But when psychologist George E. Partridge coined the term "sociopath" in 1930, he wanted it to mean, "anything deviated or pathological in social relations." In his view, the word described a pathological condition in which people are maladjusted in their relations with others and society, and motivated towards antisocial behavior.

We need this word today. We need language to describe the millions of people living among us who are socially sick, no matter what their precise diagnosis.

These disordered individuals are abusive — emotionally, psychologically, financially, physically, sexually, socially and/or spiritually. Why they are abusive varies, depending on the disorder. Antisocials and psychopaths want power and control. Narcissists believe they are the center of the universe, and should be treated that way. Borderlines feel lost and empty inside, and want someone to fill them up.

But if you're the target of their abuse, the reason for it doesn't matter. You need to ease the sociopath out of your life. And if that's not possible, you need to find ways to keep a lid on his or her exploitation.

Best of the Lovefraud Blog Series

This book will help you. It is a collection of my most popular Lovefraud Blog articles related to dealing with sociopaths.

Lovefraud has more than 4,000 blog posts. They are spread over years of archives, so articles on a particular topic are not always easy to find. Therefore, in this *Best of the Lovefraud Blog* series of books, I've collected, updated and organized hundreds

Introduction

of posts into specific themes:

- *Understanding the Sociopath*
- *Seduced by a Sociopath*
- *Dealing with a Sociopath*
- *Recovery from a Sociopath*

Dealing with a Sociopath offers tips and advice on what to do, and what not to do, when you have no choice but to interact with disordered individuals. You need to understand how they think, what they are capable of, and how best to protect yourself. Knowledge is power.

Sociopaths: The giant skeleton
in humanity's closet

Lovefraud received the following email from a reader in Holland whom we'll call "Anika:"

Today I registered to your love fraud site. Nice that you created it. It is a great help when you are abused by a socio-psychopath whatever you call it. I've been divorced from mine almost 30 years. Only 3 years ago I read a book that explained to me why, after my divorce, my life changed from a drama into a hell.

And this blog and sites are very helpful. Knowledge gives power. So I am together with a cousin (who is also divorced her psychopath), working on creating something like this in Holland. In our country it seems to be an unknown subject.

I want to write especially about the troubles the Npders can cause between the children and their mother or fathers. That's what happened in my case. My ex trained the children in abusive and cruel behavior towards me.

My son doesn't know the facts of why I divorced his father. His father (who works as a homeopathic doctor) told my kids, when they were in their puberty, that the great drama in their lives was that their mother caused them a lot of harm by having this (so called) depression after the divorce. I only found out years afterward what he did, because he never told me that he was putting this idea in their heads. (And he forgot to mention his messing around with other women and lies about that, which destroyed our marriage.)

When I asked my children if they please can explain to me what happened and how, they most of the time get very angry, start to scream at me, or walk away but cannot give any example. They avoid contact with me most of the time.

I have had no contact with my daughter for several years. One year ago I gave it another try. First by e-mail and then I paid her 2 visits that were 2 very pleasant occasions. I could feel her love, and the atmosphere was very good.

She wrote me this also in an e-mail. And then she started to create distance between her and me.

My son, luckily, has 2 kids and he likes me to be the grandmother. I am very lucky with them that contact is very good, we love each other big time.

Well that's my story in a nutshell.

Anika's story is just like many of the 10,000 stories that have been sent to Lovefraud — and that is exactly why I posted it. This story came from Europe. Sociopaths are everywhere — Lovefraud has received stories from all over the world. Sociopaths are in all demographic groups. They are male, female, rich, poor, all races, all religions and live in all communities.

Anika also said that sociopathy "seems to be an unknown subject" in Holland. Well, it's an unknown subject all around the world. Yes, we're talking about social predators here on Lovefraud, which is based in the United States, but that certainly doesn't mean Americans have any more awareness of this personality disorder than anyone else does.

Because Hollywood and the media typically portray sociopaths as deranged serial killers, our "understanding" of them may do us more harm than good. Why? When people believe sociopaths are all deranged killers, it may blind them to the fact that a lying, manipulative, abusive partner or colleague may be a sociopath. Because the individual hasn't killed anyone, it may be hard to believe that he or she has a serious personality disorder.

The fact that predators live among us is like a giant skeleton in the closet of the human race. It's a massive problem that no one wants to talk about.

Defining the problem

One reason why this huge problem remains outside of our awareness is that it is poorly defined. Even though people have been talking about evil since biblical times, there is no widely accepted definition of what it is.

In my book, *Red Flags of Love Fraud — 10 signs you're dating a sociopath,* I suggest that the word "sociopath" be used as a generic umbrella description for social predators — people who live their lives by exploiting others. Within the framework of "sociopathy," experts (who disagree on what to call this personality disorder and how it should be diagnosed) can define specific diagnoses, such as antisocial personality disorder, psychopathy, narcissism and borderline personality disorder.

Massive numbers

According to one U.S. government survey, up to 3.8% of the population have antisocial personality disorder, up to 6.2% have narcissistic personality disorder, up to 5.9% have borderline personality disorder, and up to 1.8% have histrionic personality disorder. Other estimates are lower. Averaging the figures out, approximately 12% of the people who live among us are social predators.

As of July 2012, the population of the United States was nearly 314 million. If up to 12% are sociopaths, that means there are as many as 37 million social predators in America.

The world population is almost 7 billion. If 12% are sociopaths, the total is a staggering 837 million. This is a massive problem.

So why are there 837 million disordered people in the world, exploiting almost everyone they meet, and most people don't know about it? Perhaps the whole concept is just too scary.

Cultural conspiracy

Human beings are social creatures. We live in groups and depend on each other. How do we cope with the idea that some of our own species are predators? They look like us and act like us, but their objective is not to live in community with us — it is to take advantage of us and perhaps destroy us.

Maybe we just don't want to go there. We are, after all, capable of massive conspiracy. Take Santa Claus. I've always been amazed that every adult in every country where Christmas is celebrated knows, in the presence of children, to keep the Santa Claus story going. So maybe we're living with another massive cultural conspiracy that goes something like this: All people are basically good and want the same thing is life — to love and be loved.

It's a cultural message that we hear time and time again. Unfortunately, it is not totally true. There are exceptions to this general belief in the goodness and sameness of people. The exceptions are the sociopaths.

We need to open the closet and shed light on the fact that 837 million social predators live among us. They look like us, but they do not live like us. These people do not love. They care only about power, control and manipulation.

The first step towards protecting ourselves from sociopaths is knowing that they exist.

10 mistakes to avoid when leaving a sociopath

Ending a relationship with a sociopath is not a normal break-up.

Sociopaths (people who could be diagnosed with antisocial, narcissistic, borderline, histrionic or psychopathic personality disorders) do not pursue romantic relationships in search of mutual love and companionship. They are looking for someone to use in some way — such as for money, sex, or to siphon off your emotional energy.

Therefore, when you end a relationship with a sociopath, you can't get together, hug, cry and wish each other well, as you might with a normal person. When leaving a sociopath, you need to be strategic. Here are 10 mistakes to avoid:

1. Thinking you can still be friends

You may still be cordial — even close — with past romantic partners. This doesn't work with sociopaths. If you have any contact at all, the sociopath will attempt to reel you back in and exploit you again. You need to get the person out of your life — completely and permanently.

2. Getting together in person to break up

Yes, the polite way to end a relationship is for everyone to have closure. But sociopaths don't care about closure — they care about maintaining control over you. When you're leaving a sociopath, breaking up by text — or even ghosting — is acceptable. Don't seek closure from your partner. Give it to yourself.

3. Believing that the sociopath can or will change

Remember — sociopaths are fundamentally different from the rest of us. Once they are adults, no therapy or rehabilitation will cure their disorder. Therefore, don't fall for their pleading or promises. No matter what they say, they cannot permanently change. You need to accept that and act accordingly.

4. Feeling responsible for the sociopath's behavior

After abusive behavior, the sociopath may have said, "I did that because you (insert supposed offense here)" — blaming his or her behavior on you. Don't believe it. You are not responsible for the sociopath's actions.

5. Staying to prevent the sociopath from committing suicide

If the sociopath you're breaking up with threatens suicide, he or she is either serious, or trying to make you feel guilty so that you don't leave. Either way, the best thing you can do is call 911. If the person is serious, let the professionals deal with it. If the person is not serious, you have called his or her bluff.

6. Failing to protect your physical safety

Unfortunately, some sociopaths are vindictive and violent. When someone is physically abusive, the most dangerous time for you is when you are leaving the relationship. The sociopath may fly into a rage and do the unthinkable. If you have ever seen the sociopath engage in violence, whether towards people, animals or property, take precautions.

7. Failing to lock down your finances

When sociopaths have access to your financial accounts or records, they may steal your money, run up your credit cards, or steal your identity and open accounts in your name. The first thing you should do when you leave a sociopath is run a credit check on yourself.

8. Failing to lock down your electronics

If sociopaths have had access to your cell phone, computers and other devices, they may install spyware to monitor your communications, or key loggers to steal your passwords. These can be very difficult to detect and eradicate. You may need to get all new devices.

9. Failing to understand the smear campaign

Long before you knew there were any problems in your relationship, the sociopath may have started undermining you. They often lie about you to your friends, family or even employers, accusing you of doing drugs, cheating or being mentally ill. The objective is to ruin your support network, so that when you seek help and validation, no one believes you.

10. Underestimating the sociopathic desire for revenge

Many sociopaths (especially narcissists, antisocials, borderlines and psychopaths) view romantic rejection as a "narcissistic injury" — a totally unacceptable affront to their egos. They may decide that the person who caused the injury (you) must be punished. If you think this may happen, plan your exit with caution.

When sociopaths lie about you

It's bad enough that sociopaths lie to hook you. Anything they tell you about themselves may be false — their age, education, credentials, family details, income, criminal record or employment.

And of course, sociopaths typically lie about their relationship history and status. They claim to be single when they are married; they claim to be childless when they have many offspring — even with multiple partners.

Sociopaths lie — it's the key characteristic of the disorder. When you fall for the lies, you feel like a chump. But what often turns out to be even more devastating is the lies they tell about you.

The smear campaign

Sociopaths typically engage in a "smear campaign" about their targets. These are outright lies that they tell about you to your family, friends, neighbors, co-workers and others in your social circle.

The sociopath's objective with the smear campaign is to compromise your social support system, and therefore increase his or her control over you. For this reason, the sociopath may start lying about you long before you suspect any problems in your relationship.

For example, a sociopath may have a conversation like the following with your friend, Jane:

Sociopath: "You know, I found out about six months into our relationship that Mary was cheating on me. She was secretly seeing a guy from work."

Jane: "I never knew about that!"

Sociopath: "Well, I imagine that she didn't want to tell you, because you might have said something to me. I know I can trust you."

Jane: "Of course you can!"

Sociopath: "I really love Mary, so I've forgiven her."

You, of course, never cheated on the sociopath — the entire story is complete fabrication. But look at what happens because of what the sociopath said:

- Jane thinks you cheated on your partner, which lowers her opinion of you.
- Jane believes you are keeping secrets from her, so you aren't much of a friend.
- The sociopath pretends to be wronged, which elicits sympathy from Jane.
- The sociopath enlists Jane as a potential informer.
- For taking you back after you supposedly cheated, the sociopath claims the moral high ground.

All of these dynamics may be very useful to the sociopath down the road, when you split up and find that your family and friends are supporting him rather than you.

The top lie

I've heard from many, many people that sociopaths have accused them of being crazy, psycho, unbalanced, needing therapy or needing medication. So I think the most prevalent lies sociopaths tell about you are statements undermining your mental stability.

What's really dangerous about these statements is the manner in which they are said. Instead of ranting about you, often sociopaths seem to be expressing concern.

A sociopath will quietly say to your friends and family, "You know, I'm really worried about Mary. She really seems to be losing it. But she just won't go see a therapist."

They come across as so believable.

You, of course, may be legitimately suffering from anxiety or depression because of emotional and psychological abuse by the sociopath. And due to the sociopath's gaslighting, you may even be questioning your own sanity.

Still, by questioning your mental ability to your family and friends, the sociopath weakens your standing and makes them less likely to support your decisions. The sociopath, in the meantime, is seen as a concerned partner, someone who is looking out for your well-being, which couldn't be further from the truth.

Picking your battles

Sometimes the sociopath's smear campaign has been going on for so long, and has been so well orchestrated, that you may find your entire family, social group or community aligned against you. I've heard from many people who realize that everyone in their church believes the sociopath's lies and not them.

This is terribly distressing. Your reputation is shredded, and you did nothing wrong. So how do you fight this? What do you do?

Unfortunately, sociopaths are such accomplished liars that some people will believe their stories no matter how much you protest. So here's what I suggest:

Figure out which people are really important to you and need to know the truth. Do your best to tell them your side of the story. Show them proof if you have it.

For everyone else, you develop a stock response, perhaps a shrug and, "He likes to tell stories."

You may find that you will need to walk away from some people, remove them from your life. So be it.

When to fight

There is one situation in which you must do your best to fight the lies: When you have a court case involving a sociopath.

Sociopaths have absolutely no qualms about lying in court testimony or court documents. When the sociopaths lie about you in court, you MUST object.

Court proceedings are all about establishing a "record." Because everything said during a court proceeding is supposed to be the truth, sociopaths are assumed to be telling the truth, no matter what they say. So when their statements are lies, you must counter them.

If you fail to dispute the sociopaths' lies, they become part of the court record. This can turn into a real problem later on.

Another time to fight is when you are accused of a crime that you did not do. You may be advised to plead guilty, especially if you can't afford a lawyer. This is generally a bad idea. A guilty plea means a criminal record, and a criminal record will cause you big problems later in life.

3 questions to help you respond

Here's the bottom line: Sociopaths lie about everything, so they are likely to lie about you. No one wants to be characterized falsely. But realize that you can choose how, or even if, you will respond to the lies.

Here are three questions to help you decide what to do:

1. Does this particular lie damage my life?
2. Does this person need to know the truth?
3. Will responding to the lie keep me engaged with the sociopath?

In situations where you can move on without combating the lie, that might be the best approach. Reserve your energy for taking action on the matters that are vital to your life.

10 tactics for child custody battles with sociopaths

L ast week Dr. Liane Leedom wrote about the tragic case Dr. Amy Castillo, whose children were murdered by their psychopathic father after several judges issued rulings that failed to protect them. I hope this terrible and extreme case will be a wake-up call for family courts.

Lovefraud frequently receives email from men and women involved in child custody disputes with sociopaths, who, hopefully, are not murderers. Here is one of them:

> I am involved in a custody case with a sociopath, however, my case is being fought in Europe where I recently relocated to (I am American, he is European). After being the sole caregiver of my children for five years, I had no choice but to leave them with their father and return to the States. When we separated he took their passports and left the country for a year. It was NOT possible to obtain new passports for children without BOTH parents' signatures.
>
> By the end of that year my financial situation was desperate and I had no choice. I came back to the States, got myself back on my feet and recently I started my own company as a Virtual Assistant, allowing me to work anywhere in the world. While in the States I came back to Europe every six to eight weeks to visit my children. Well one month ago, I relocated back to Europe to live and continue

my fight for custody of my children.

The court case had already been ongoing since January and in typical sociopath style he has lied and forged documents. Even so, my ex was recently given sole custody (temporarily while custody is decided) and that I must pay him 900 euros (around $1,300 USD a month!). As if that could not be bad enough, he sends me on a regular basis (the most recent being today) faxes full of lies and accusations that he then turns around and uses as evidence in his court case!!! Furthermore, I do NOT have 900 euros a month to give him. I just relocated and started my own business and this is a real slap in the face with all of the financial damage he has done to me as well as my credit in the U.S.

I have fired my attorneys and hired the best Custody/Family attorney where I live. He has been in practice for 30 years and not has lost a case! Also he is known to be a very strong and tough attorney. I wish I would have had him in the beginning. So with this I feel confidence.

The reason I am writing is because although I have a very positive outlook and feel that I am a strong person, as I know that most of you can agree, it is very difficult dealing with a sociopath. When I receive these horrible faxes my stomach just drops and it can make me feel very anxious for hours after. So now I have stopped reading them at all. I do not know what I am looking for by sending this email. I think I just need the support of knowing there are others out there going through the same things as me and that this is manageable and that I will make it through. I would greatly appreciate hearing what others have done in a situation like this. Thank you.

Like most parents fighting a custody battle with a sociopath, this woman faces a difficult times. Below are some general suggestions about child custody and sociopaths.

Get him or her to walk away

If your ex is a sociopath, at best, he or she will be a lousy parent. At worst, he or she will intentionally try to damage your children. Therefore, if at all possible, it may be best to cut the sociopath out of your children's lives.

You may want to consider offering the sociopath an incentive to walk away. Tell the sociopath to give up parental rights, and he or she won't have to pay any child support. You may feel that you need the child support payments, but chances are that you'll never get the money, or it will always be a struggle to get it. The money isn't worth having the predator in your family's life. Figure out a way to support your children without it.

Sometimes this works—there are sociopaths who care more about money than kids. But many times it doesn't, because the sociopath considers children to be possessions. Or, the sociopath just wants to win the battle with you, and destroy you in the process. In those cases, you'll end up in court.

Tactics in custody battles

I am forever grateful that I never had children with my sociopathic ex-husband. I avoided the most tragic of circumstances involving these predators—a child custody battle. Therefore, the suggestions I make below come from my research and what Lovefraud readers have told me.

If you're fighting a custody battle with a sociopath, here are some tactics to follow:

1. Document, document, document.

Keep a journal of everything that happens. Often, the craziness is so intense that you don't want to remember what happens. Your journal will be important when you need to tell a cohesive story of what has been going on with the sociopath, especially if you need to tell it long after events have transpired. Save every scrap of paper, every email, every fax, every receipt. Develop a way of organizing the information, whether chronological, or by topic. Keep copies in a safe place.

2. Have witnesses

It is best not to deal with the sociopath alone; every interaction then becomes he said/she said. Have a trusted friend or relative present during child exchanges or other interactions as much as you can. You may even want to consider tape recording and video-taping some of what goes on.

3. Get your own information

Do not allow the sociopathic parent to control information about your children. Make sure you get information directly from schools, doctors and others.

4. Hire an aggressive, competent attorney

Child custody cases with sociopaths are not normal cases. The sociopath will not play by the rules. Your attorney must understand this. The sociopath will lie in court, although his or her performance will appear heartfelt, like he or she is "just concerned with the welfare of the children." The sociopath will make outrageous accusations. The sociopath is also likely to retain an attorney who is also sociopathic. Therefore, your attorney must be up for the challenge.

5. Do not allow lies to become part of the court record

Sociopaths lie. Sociopaths lie convincingly. You cannot allow unchallenged lies to become part of the court records. Once they are, they take on the aura of truth, and put you in a very bad position. Some lies, like accusations of child abuse, may haunt you forever.

6. Be cautious in stating that your ex is, in fact, a sociopath

Unfortunately, many judges really do not understand what this means to the welfare of a child. Like the general public, many judges equate "sociopath" with "serial killer," and may consequently believe that you are overreacting. So it may not be in your best interest to prove that he or she is a sociopath. Focus on proving the behavior.

7. Stay calm in court

You must present a calm, professional image when you go to court, even as the sociopath lies. Do not allow the sociopath to make you emotional. The sociopath will accuse you of being unstable, and you will prove it by your behavior in court. Keep your emotions in check, at least in front of the judge.

8. Make sure court orders are explicit

Insist on detailed court orders. The order should not say, "parent has visitation every other weekend." It should specify exactly which weekends, starting at what times, returning at what times, who is responsible for transporting children, who is responsible for bathing and feeding them—everything must be spelled out in detail. If there is any ambiguity, the sociopath will exploit it.

9. Make the sociopath abide by court orders

If the sociopath fails to honor the orders, do not cut him or her any slack. Record any violation. Call the police if necessary. Continue to document everything that happens, because you may need to go to court again. If you ever decide that you need to cut the sociopath out of the child's life, you'll need evidence to do it.

10. Take care of yourself

You will need all your resources to deal with the sociopath. Therefore, make healthy decisions in your own life. Eat right, avoid drugs and alcohol, get enough sleep, exercise and develop a support network. In order to care for your children, you must care for yourself.

7 reasons why regular people enable sociopaths

Three former administration officials of Penn State University were sentenced to jail last Friday because they failed to report signs that Jerry Sandusky, the former assistant football coach, was sexually abusing boys.

This is right and just. They should be held accountable.

The former university president, Graham B. Spanier, will spend at least two months in jail, followed by two months of house arrest. Gary Schultz, the former athletic director, and Tim Curley, a former vice president, will also spend time in jail, followed by house arrest.

On October 9, 2012, Sandusky was sentenced to 30 to 60 years in prison for assaulting 10 boys. However, more men also came forward, and Penn State offered settlements to approximately 30 victims.

Penn State University has paid out nearly $250 million in settlements, legal bills, fines, public relations and other costs as a result of the scandal. Much of this would have been avoided if the administrators had acted appropriately when they learned about Sandusky's behavior.

The Philadelphia Inquirer quoted Prosecutor Laura Ditka's statement about the president, Spanier:

"He was a complete and utter failure as a leader when it mattered the most," Ditka said during Friday's hearing. "He made the choice to protect his reputation, the reputation of his friends and the reputation of the university above the well-being of these children. And that is inexcusable."

Read complete coverage on Philly.com, *Penn State's Spanier gets jail for role in Sandusky scandal.*

Jerry Sandusky is antisocial (although as part of his defense he said he suffered from histrionic personality disorder). The three university officials failed to do what was right when they became aware of his sexual abuse, and therefore enabled Sandusky to keep on preying on boys.

Unfortunately, plenty of normally good, upright people fail to take action when we become aware of sociopathic manipulation, exploitation, and crimes. Here are seven reasons why.

1. We lack awareness about sociopathic behavior

This is a major blind spot that applies to almost everyone — including all of us, before our personal encounters with sociopaths.

Society teaches us that we're all created equal, we're all God's children, we all just want to be loved, and everyone has good inside. This is true for 88% of the population. But no one tells us about the approximately 12% of the population — those with exploitative personality disorders, for whom none of these platitudes apply.

Therefore, even when we see evidence of any kind of abusive behavior, we doubt ourselves. We can't imagine that the people are actually doing what we think they are doing. We must be wrong, we must be imagining things, so we do nothing.

2. We are deceived

Sociopaths lie. They lie a lot. They lie about incidents large and small. Unfortunately, for a very long time, we don't know that they are lying.

This is especially true because sociopaths engage in impression management. In the beginning of any kind of involvement, they are friendly, helpful, charming, reliable and thoughtful.

They are creating a trustworthy image. We see the behavior, and because all human beings are designed to trust, we have no reason to second-guess the authenticity of their actions.

So when sociopaths make the switch, and embark on manipulation and exploitation, we are pre-programmed with their trust-worthy image, and assume the bad behavior must be some kind of mistake.

3. We want to protect an organization or institution

This is clearly what happened in the Penn State case — jurors were shown emails that prosecutors said the three administrators hatched a plan to keep the issue quiet.

This also happens in the cases of military spouse abuse. When wives, and some husbands, are abandoned, military commanders have an obligation to make sure the soldier does what he is supposed to do for his family. But many commanders are more focused on the mission and the reputation of the services. If some individuals are getting trampled in the meantime, well, that's just too bad.

In any kind of cover-up, doing what's right loses out to doing what's good for a certain person, group or organization.

4. We don't want to get involved

We all have our own issues and problems. Making a report may mean that we become involved with a criminal or legal matter, or with someone else's problems. We tell ourselves that we simply don't have the time or energy for another situation.

It's easier to just stay out of it.

5. We fall for the spin

Perhaps we actually stage an intervention about the sociopath's unacceptable behavior. Immediately, the sociopaths start spinning it. They have excuses; they have reasons; they tell you it's not what it appears to be.

Or, they admit the error of their ways, and promise to change. And they may appear to change — for a little while.

We don't really want a partner, friend or co-worker to get in trouble — we just want them to stop the abuse. So we fall for the spin and give them another chance. Eventually, however, the bad behavior resumes. In fact, it may be worse than ever.

6. We are caught in the web

Sociopaths are expert at pulling people into their plots and conspiracies. Of course, they do not announce their intentions. They draw us in bit by bit. Sociopaths convince us to overlook one thing, and then something else. They push us to violate a boundary, and then another one. Before we know it, we are in over our heads.

This is a standard practice when sociopaths are bleeding us for money. They borrow a little bit, and may actually pay it back, in order to establish trust. Then they keep asking for money — not for themselves, of course, but because there is some crisis that requires cash to fix.

When the bank account is empty, they ask about credit cards. Or a second mortgage. Or borrowing money from friends and family.

Then we realize something illicit is going on. But if we report the matter, we ourselves are complicit.

7. We fear retribution

Sooner or later, we learn that sociopaths are highly vindictive. If we take a stand against them, we know that their wrath will be turned on us.

This often happens in divorce and child custody situations. This partner who was once so loving becomes the most vile person in the world. There is no amicable split. There is no doing what's best for the kids.

Many sociopaths approach divorce with scorched earth tactics. They don't just want to leave you; they want to crush you. And typically, they've been planning their escape long before you even knew there was a problem, so they've depleted the money, eroded your support system and perhaps even framed you for crimes.

You may want to do what's right, but the sociopath doesn't. So all you can do is figure out how to survive.

How to stop enabling

The key to putting an end to enabling behavior is to under-

35

stand that a sociopath, once an adult, will not change. It doesn't matter how much we cajole or appease, the sociopath will continue to exploit and manipulate.

Therefore, enabling behavior like those listed above may work in the short term, but over time, they are likely to backfire — as it did in the Penn State case. Therefore, the sooner enabling stops, the better.

Do not marry a murderer

William Balfour, 31, of Chicago, was found guilty last week of murdering Darnell Donerson, Jason Hudson and Julian King. They were the mother, brother and nephew of singer and actress Jennifer Hudson.

In my opinion, this case was a tragedy, but a preventable tragedy. Julia Hudson, Jennifer's older sister, brought Balfour into the family when she married him. If she hadn't married this man, it obviously wouldn't have happened.

Jennifer Hudson was the first witness in the murder trial. She testified that the entire family was against Julia's relationship with Balfour. "None of us wanted her to marry him. We did not like how he treated her," she stated in court.

Julia secretly married William Balfour anyway in December 2006.

Who is William Balfour?

William Balfour is one of those people who was dealt a bad hand in life, and made it worse.

It seems that his family history includes sociopathy. His father was convicted of murder and sentenced to 30 years. His maternal grandmother went to prison for manslaughter. His mother was physically abusive to Balfour and his older brother.

Balfour himself had an extensive juvenile record, ran away from shelters and relatives' homes, dropped out of school in ninth grade and joined a gang. At age 17, he stole a car with the owner clinging to the hood and crashed it into a telephone pole. He was convicted of attempted murder.

Hook up

When William Balfour got out of prison in 2006, he hooked up with Julia Hudson, whom he knew from elementary school.

I can imagine how that seduction went:

"Julia, baby, you are so fine — if I was with a woman like you, I could turn my life around — you know I never had a chance — my dad was locked up as long as I can remember — my mom used to beat me and my brother — she actually gave us up, said she didn't want us around any more — mothers are supposed to love you, but my mother never showed me any love — you're a woman who knows how to love, I can just tell —yeah, I used to be wild, but I did my time, and now I'm ready for a new life — with you at my side, I'll be a new man — I know I can do it — c'mon, baby, I really want to make something of myself — but I can't do it without you — you know I love you, and you love me — there's no reason for us to wait."

I'm sure Balfour laid it on thick. He probably anticipated that if he hooked up with Julia Hudson, he'd be on the gravy train, because Julia's sister was an actress — a movie star — a celebrity — and rich.

When Julia Hudson no longer wanted Balfour around, my guess is that not only was he outraged to lose control of her, but he was also outraged to lose the gravy train.

Reasons

Yes, William Balfour never had a chance in life. I recognize that he came from the mean streets of Chicago, as did Julia Hudson. She could have felt sorry for him. But she didn't have to marry him.

Many Lovefraud readers have accepted as romantic partners people with serious life issues—including arrests, convictions, addictions and other problems. Why did they do it? Here are some of the reasons I've heard:

- Everyone deserves a second chance.
- I felt sorry for him (her).
- I believed I could change him (her).
- I just knew there was a good person inside him (her).
- I believe in the power of love.
- I'm a Christian, and I believe people can repent.
- He (she) needed me.
- He (she) just needed unconditional love.

The relationships were disastrous. No matter how much unconditional love was provided, it was overwhelmed by manipulation, deceit and exploitation.

Disqualifications for marriage

The purpose of marriage is a life partnership, in which both spouses support each other. Marriage is not social work. Therefore, if you are searching for a spouse, I recommend eliminating anyone with the following characteristics or history:

1. Conviction for murder or attempted murder
2. History of domestic violence
3. Conviction for fraud, theft or property crimes
4. Drug dealing or manufacturing
5. No apparent income or means of financial support
6. Pathological lying
7. Failure to support children
8. Controlling behavior
9. Outbursts of rage
10. Suffered abuse as a child, combined with any of the above.

Do not delude yourself into thinking that your relationship will be different, your love is special, you can change the person. Yes, sometimes people can turn themselves around. But do you want to bet your life on this person, and the lives of your family and friends?

Game theory and the sociopath

Shock. Total disbelief. Utter incomprehension. That's what we feel upon finally realizing that when the sociopath cheated on us, blew through our money, twisted our emotions and messed with our minds, to him or her it was all just a sick, depraved game.

Sociopaths do not form emotional connections with other human beings. They do not experience love. They do not feel honor, altruism or concern for others. The words they speak and the actions they take have only one objective: getting what they want. To them, life is a game, and they want to win.

Game theory is a field of study that, according to Wikipedia, "attempts to mathematically capture behavior in strategic situations, in which an individual's success in making choices depends on the choices of others."

Sociopaths are often very good at games in this sense. They look at social situations, perform a quick cost-benefit analysis, and then act based on what will serve their interests. For example, a sociopath may evaluate a situation like this: "If I tell her that I love her, and promise to marry her, she'll let me move in and give me money to pay off my back child support so the court will get off my back." Notice there is no love, no concern for children. It's all about a means to an end.

Prisoner's Dilemma

According to game theory, many variables can affect outcomes in contested situations. For example, people are generally, although not always, assumed to be rational and making choices that benefit their own self-interest. It's also important for participants to know whether another player in the game can be trusted, or is likely to be deceptive.

A famous game in this field of study is called the "Prisoner's Dilemma." Here, according to Wikipedia, is the classic scenario:

> Two suspects are arrested by the police. The police have insufficient evidence for a conviction, and, having separated both prisoners, visit each of them to offer the same deal. If one testifies (defects from the other) for the prosecution against the other and the other remains silent (cooperates with the other), the betrayer goes free and the silent accomplice receives the full 10-year sentence. If both remain silent, both prisoners are sentenced to only six months in jail for a minor charge. If each betrays the other, each receives a five-year sentence. Each prisoner must choose to betray the other or to remain silent. Each one is assured that the other would not know about the betrayal before the end of the investigation. How should the prisoners act?

The choice, therefore, is between cooperation and defection. In studies, players have participated in a variation of the Prisoner's Dilemma in which they earned points based on their choices. The possible outcomes were:

- If both players cooperated, they each earned 3 points.
- If both players defected, they each earned 1 point.
- If one player cooperated and the other player defected, the cooperating player got 0 points—the sucker punch—and the defecting player got 5 points.

Therefore, when one person cooperated and the other defected, the defector came out way ahead.

Reputation

Psychology researcher Linda Mealey published a paper in 1995 called *The Sociobiology of Sociopathy: An Integrated Evolutionary Model*. In it, she discussed another dimension of the Prisoner's Dilemma game as it applies to real life. If the most rational strategy is to be selfish and betray, why would anyone cooperate?

The answer lies in reputation. If a player is known among members of a group to always defect, then no rational person will "play" with him or her. When a person has a reputation as a defector, that person will not have an opportunity for any kind of gain, cooperative or exploitative.

This is where game theory becomes useful in dealing with sociopaths. Mealey writes:

> Sociopaths' immediate decisions are based partly on their ability to use those expectations of others' behavior in a cost-benefit analysis to assess what actions are likely to be in their own self-interest. The outcome of such analyses is therefore partially dependent on the sociopath's expectations of the behavior of other players in the game. I would argue that an entire society can be seen as a player, and that the past behavior of that society will be used by the sociopath to predict the future behavior of that society.
>
> Like an individual player, a society will have a certain probability of detecting deception, a more-or-less accurate memory of who has cheated in the past, and a certain proclivity to retaliate or not, based upon a cheater's past reputation and current behavior. Since the sociopath is using a rational and actuarial approach to assess the costs and benefits of different behaviors, it is the actual past behavior of the society which will go into his calculations, rather than risk assessments inflated from the exaggerated fears or anxieties that most people feel in anticipation of being caught or punished. Thus, to reduce antisocial behavior, a society must establish and enforce a reputation

for high rates of detection of deception and identification of cheaters, and a willingness to retaliate. In other words, it must establish a successful strategy of deterrence.

According to Mealey, a society "must establish a reputation for willingness to retaliate." This means increasing the probability of criminal detection, identification and punishment. And the retaliation must be swift. If there's a long lag time between antisocial behavior and consequences—well, the antisocial behavior will continue.

Exposure

Mealey's comments related to reputation square with what I have seen. Since our society hasn't established a reputation for willingness to retaliate—the justice system is a joke—the only effective action to take against sociopaths is exposure.

The case histories section of Lovefraud, called True Lovefraud Stories, exposes the behavior of 23 different sociopaths. It works. I've heard from many people who came in contact with the predators, Googled them, found the Lovefraud stories, and dumped the sociopath. One woman, discovering what Bill Strunk was really all about, actually told him that he had a "bad reputation."

Lovefraud's goal for the future is to publish many more bad reputations. Hopefully, then, people won't play with the sociopaths.

Advice for dealing with sociopaths: Don't take it personally

Lovefraud received this note from a reader; we'll call her "Allison."

> I want to thank everyone involved with the Lovefraud website. It is truly a gift. To the brave survivors, I wish you peace. I am a survivor myself. In fact, I'm divorcing mine as we speak. I will write my story another time because this time I only want to give a piece of advice that has helped me the most. When I was able to do this, the rest was easier to get through. I stopped taking it personally. It was not an easy task. I read everything I could get my hands on and while I learned his actions were mostly textbook, it was easier for me to let go. Once I convinced myself that I was not the first nor will I be the last, I shut my heart off and stopped taking it personally. This was my key to survival. I offered a silent apology to the women of the world for throwing this one back into the dating pool and went on with my life. I stopped taking it personally and I slept better, dreamed better, laughed more and found that I'll be just fine. If this helps even one person, it will have made it worth it. Take care.

Allison's advice is very simple, but it goes directly to the core of the sociopath's manipulation, betrayal and abuse. The sociopath never cared about us one way or the other. We were convenient targets. We had something the sociopath wanted. Or we presented an opportunity for the sociopath's amusement.

Sociopaths do what they do, because that's what they do. We just happened to be there.

Of course, that's not what the sociopath told us. First, he or she proclaimed love and devotion, or a sterling opportunity to succeed together — whatever the promise was. Then, when the promise started falling apart, the sociopath told us it was all our fault.

We, as normal human beings, believed the original promise — how could anyone say those words and not mean them? So, when the blame started flying from the person who made the promise, we believed that as well.

As we say here on Lovefraud, the sociopath is the lie. And the sociopath lied because that's what they do. They are missing the parts — emotional connections to other people and conscience — that make us human.

Opportunity for healing

Still, there is a reason that we went along with the sociopath's program, and that is something we do need to take personally, for our own recovery and growth.

This does not at all excuse the sociopath's heartless behavior, nor is it meant to blame the victim. But most of us engaged because we wanted to believe the original promise.

We have to ask ourselves, what was missing within us that allowed us to believe? Did we have experiences in our past that made us susceptible to the manipulation? If so, it's time to look at these issues and heal ourselves.

So as we extricate ourselves from the sociopath, understand that this is how they are, their behavior is not our fault, and we shouldn't take it personally.

But we should take very personally the opportunity to excavate the old, erroneous tapes in our heads, and create wonderful new lives for ourselves.

What NOT to do when you realize you're involved with a sociopath

You've been living in insanity. Your partner seems to randomly lash out or give you the silent treatment, and then says you're to blame. Your finances are in shambles, and you're to blame for that too — even if you're the only one working. You are positive that this person is cheating on you, but he or she insists you are paranoid and delusional.

Or, in a variation on a theme, you are living with the distinct feeling that something is amiss, although you can't quite figure out what it is.

You Google terms like "emotional abuse" or "signs of cheating" or "love and deceit." Eventually you end up on Lovefraud.

Suddenly, everything makes sense. The articles describe what you're experiencing. Other people are telling stories that sound just like yours.

You realize that you're involved with a sociopath.

You are horrified — this personality disorder sounds really, really bad, and there is no treatment for it.

But you are also relieved — now you know you are not crazy; it's him (or her).

So what do you do with this information?

First, here's what NOT to do: Do NOT confront the sociopath.

Even though you want to say, "I KNOW WHAT YOU ARE!!!"

Even though you want to defend yourself, "IT'S NOT ME, IT'S YOU!!!"

Don't do it.

Now that you know what you're dealing with, keep the information to yourself and carefully plan what you're going to do next.

The sociopath's reaction

Sociopaths are all about power and control. If you tell the person that you have figured out that everything he or she has told you is a lie, that everything he or she has done was manipulation, the sociopath will perceive a loss of power and control over you.

The sociopath will probably react in one of these ways:

Love bombing: He or she will turn on the charm or plead for another chance, causing you to doubt yourself and drawing you back into the web.

Rage: He or she will become infuriated and ratchet up the abuse.

Abandonment: He or she will abruptly leave, causing as much damage to you as possible on the way out.

Any of these reactions by the sociopath will probably make your situation more difficult.

So even though you now know the truth, put on an act. Pretend that everything is the same, while you evaluate the extent of the sociopath's deceit and exploitation. Figure out how you are going to extricate yourself from the involvement to best protect your safety, health, finances and reputation.

Sociopath's family

Here's something else you should NOT do: Do not confide in the sociopath's family.

Keep in mind that this disorder is highly genetic, so it is quite possible that the sociopath's parents, siblings or other relatives are also disordered. If so, they will side with the sociopath to help him or her keep control over you.

Or, the family may be clueless. Some family members — especially if they don't see the sociopath very often — may have absolutely no idea what he or she is really like. If the sociopath starts playing the victim, they may buy the act and do everything they can to help the sociopath, not you.

Or, the family may have known all along that the sociopath was no good, and wanted you to take the problem off of their hands. They don't want to deal with the disorder again, so they may sabotage your efforts to escape.

Talking to friends

Do NOT relay your suspicions to any friends who are also the sociopath's friends.

Sociopaths engage in impression management. Just as the sociopath was able to charm you for so long, he or she charms other people. So people who know the sociopath may have a hard time believing what you are saying.

This is especially true if the sociopath has already launched a smear campaign.

Long before you have any clue what is going on, the sociopath may have started laying the groundwork to discredit you. He or she may have made up stories about your behavior, or "confided" that you're "mentally unstable."

The sociopath may have subtly turned people against you. So if you start talking about what has really been going on in your life, they are primed to disbelieve you.

In fact, you should also be careful about talking to your own friends.

The sociopath may contact them behind your back and convincingly express concern about you. What the sociopath really wants is information. Your friends may fall for the scam — after all, you did — and tell the sociopath something that can jeopardize your plans.

People don't understand

Keep in mind that most people simply don't understand what the words "sociopath" and "psychopath" mean. Most people think they are serial killers.

If you say you're involved with a sociopath, and that person doesn't look like a killer, others may think you're exaggerating.

So even if you're bursting to confront the sociopath, and you want to tell the world that he or she is a lying, manipulative exploiter, it's best to be very cautious about sharing the information.

Keep quiet, at least in the beginning — until you know whom you can really trust.

20 issues to consider before taking a sociopath to court

Lovefraud recently received the following email from a reader with some important questions:

> I was previously married to a sociopath, and we have a 4-year old son together. I have sole legal and physical custody of our son, but have been fighting to reduce the amount of visitation for quite some time. I recently read that having a forensic psychological analysis done on the entire family would reveal that my ex is a sociopath and possibly prevent him from having ANY visitation going forward. Is this true, in your experience? Do you have any advice for me as I embark on this process?

Many, many Lovefraud readers have realized — to their horror — that they've had a child or children with a sociopath. Once you realize that your former partner has a serious personality disorder, and that this person is incapable of feeling love, even for the children, your natural instinct is to want to protect the children from him or her.

Figuring out how to do it, however, is incredibly difficult. Following is a list of points to consider whenever you are contemplating legal action regarding your sociopathic partner and children.

The sociopath

1. The sociopath's objective is to win — whatever he or she re-

gards to be winning at the time. It may mean not only winning the court battle, but winning in a way that leaves you crushed, broken and destitute.

2. The sociopath is capable of doing absolutely anything in order to win. This includes lying under oath, accusing you of doing things that you never did, convincing other people to lie (knowingly or unknowingly), falsifying documents, threatening you and the children, and more.

3. Sociopaths often love going to court. For them it's great drama, an opportunity to be on stage, and they are terrific actors. Sociopaths can break into tears, crying about how much they love and miss the children, even though they totally ignored the kids while you all lived together, or perhaps even abused them. They can discuss your "mental problems" in a voice dripping with concern, even though the only thing wrong with you is him — or her.

4. Sociopaths usually pursue child custody for one or both of these reasons: They want to maintain control over you by controlling the kids, or they don't want to pay you child support.

5. A typical sociopathic strategy is to keep dragging you into court simply to cost you money. The idea is to bleed your finances until you can no longer afford to fight.

The law

6. Here's information from the U.S. Department of Health and Human Services:

> The 14th Amendment to the U.S. Constitution protects the fundamental liberty interest of natural parents in the care, custody, and management of their children. This protection does not disappear simply because they have not been model parents or have lost custody of a child temporarily.

Know that if you're attempting to keep your partner away from the children, Constitutional Law is not on your side.

7. No provision in the Constitution says children are entitled to loving care, or even safety, from their parents.

Judges

8. In Family Court, judges are the kings, and you are a serf. Judges have wide discretion to decide what will happen to you, your kids and your money. Their decisions are law, and other judges are loath to change or reverse any court ruling.

9. Most judges do not understand sociopaths and how they behave (just like everyone else in the world — including you before you met your partner). Many judges believe that sociopaths are hardened criminal or murderers. So if you say that your partner is a sociopath, and he or she hasn't killed anyone, the judge will likely think that you are exaggerating and are simply being vindictive against your former partner.

10. Most judges, like most people, believe that children should have both of their parents, so they often want to keep both parents in the lives of children. Even if a sociopath has physically abused the spouse, if the children themselves haven't been injured, and sometimes even if they have been injured, judges may not keep the kids away from the abuser.

11. Numerous scientific studies seem to "prove" that children do better when both parents are in their lives. Unfortunately, most of these studies do not consider whether a parent is disordered. On the other hand, there is very little research indicating that sociopaths make terrible parents. So you may go to all the trouble of proving your ex is a sociopath, only to have the judge say, "So? That doesn't make him (or her) a bad parent."

12. You can line up all your proof, evidence and psychological reports — and a judge can disregard all of it, deciding your case the way he or she wants to.

13. For all of these reasons, who you get as a judge matters a lot. When you know whom your judge is, you should find out everything you can about him or her. They are supposed to be impartial, but that isn't always the case. Some judges are biased against men. Some are biased against women. Some judges will listen to kids, some will not. This person holds your fate in his or her hands. If you know the judge you will be dealing with, take that into consideration before deciding how to proceed in any matter.

Lawyers

14. Be very, very careful about choosing a lawyer. Some lawyers are dedicated to serving their clients. But some lawyers are only interested in making money. You should shop around and get referrals — preferably from someone with a case like yours. If you feel at all uncomfortable with a lawyer, or if you feel that the person does not believe or respect you, do not retain that lawyer.

15. In dealing with a sociopath, lawyers must be up for the challenge. They must understand that the sociopath will stall, delay, fail to produce documents and ignore court orders. Lawyers should never assume that sociopaths are going to do what they're supposed to do. Sociopaths believe that the rules do not apply to them.

16. Somehow, many sociopaths manage to find sociopathic lawyers. This means not only will the sociopath do anything in order to win, but so will the lawyer.

The court industry

17. The court sometimes isn't just the court — it's an entire network of psychologists, experts, guardians ad litem, parenting coordinators and others. In some cases, all these people just keep each other in business at your expense. (Read yesterday's article: *Connecticut parents say court-ordered expenses bankrupt them.*)

18. Research shows that whoever pays for a report gets the report that they want.

Psychologists and other experts

19. Many psychologists do not understand sociopaths. They do not understand the experience of being targeted by a sociopath. They do not understand how sociopaths affect children. If you are going to retain a psychologist, make sure they get it.

20. Sociopaths are quite capable of manipulating psychologists. Sociopaths can play the victim, talk about loving their children, paint you as the person with problems — and some psychologists will swallow it all, hook, line and sinker.

Justice may not prevail

For all of these reasons, you need to have your eyes wide open before making any decision about embarking on a court action. You cannot assume that your experience in court will be about doing what is right, discovering the truth or protecting the children.

Going to court is always a crapshoot. It may cost you thousands and thousands of dollars, and you may end up with nothing.

Therefore, pick your court battles carefully.

Classic sociopathic control strategy: Accusing you of cheating

I was sitting at my kitchen table one day during my marriage to the sociopath, James Montgomery. We were arguing — I don't remember what about; we argued a lot. All of a sudden, Montgomery accused me of sleeping with another man.

I was shocked.

I had been friends with the man for about 15 years before I even met Montgomery. We were good friends. But that's all — friends. Still, Montgomery raged at me, "I know you had sex with him."

I denied this, vociferously. Montgomery kept accusing — but eventually backed down.

The accusation came out of thin air. I hadn't even seen my friend in months. So why did Montgomery do this?

Sociopaths assume everyone cheats

First of all, most sociopaths cheat. I would say that all sociopaths cheat, but a few people have told me that the sociopaths they were with did not cheat. Maybe it's true, or maybe those sociopaths were just really good at hiding it.

Anyway, sociopaths cannot love. They do not feel empathy, loyalty or remorse. But they want sex — lots of sex, with lots of variety. So even when they have a partner, sociopaths cheat, without any qualms. And since they cheat, they assume everybody else cheats also.

Asserting control

But that's not the prime reason why Montgomery accused me of sleeping with my friend. His true purpose was to assert control over me.

Had I admitted to sex with this man, Montgomery would have held it over me forever. He would have used it to prove my unworthiness and besmirch my character.

And this accusation would have been just the beginning. He would have accused me of other things as well, in an effort to tear me down mentally and emotionally. His objective? To make me more controllable.

Isolation

A sociopath may rage that you're cheating with your co-workers, neighbors, parents from your kids' sports teams. Even if you're totally innocent, and you've never even spoken to any of these people, the tirades may be almost unbearable.

So what do you do? You may try to avoid the sociopath's rage by making sure that you don't give him or her any reason to make the wild accusations. You don't talk to anyone at work. You limit contact with your neighbors or other parents.

In other words, you isolate yourself — and isolation places you further under the sociopath's control.

Warning sign

So if a partner who exhibits sociopathic traits unjustifiably accuses you of cheating, recognize the accusation for what it is — a tactic for asserting control over you. It's a warning sign that you should get out of the relationship as soon as you can.

Do not admit to cheating that you didn't do, just to get the sociopath to stop raging.

In fact, don't admit to cheating even if you did do it. Any admission of guilt will make the sociopath ratchet up the abuse exponentially — and could make escaping the relationship more difficult.

Do sociopaths return?

I received an email from a Lovefraud reader who had only one question. It's a question I hear frequently: Do sociopaths return?

The answer: Some of them don't, but some of them do.

Many people who have been romantically involved with sociopaths experienced the sudden "devalue and discard." One day the sociopath loves you. The next day the sociopath tosses you aside like a used tissue and walks away, without ever looking back.

As the person left behind, you may be in shock. You may have had no idea that your partner was unhappy. You may ask yourself, did I do something wrong? Why didn't he or she say something? Can't we work this out?

You are also astounded at the callousness of your partner's behavior. All those statements of "I love you" and "we're soul mates" — did they mean nothing? After all the time you spent together, and everything you've been through, how can this person just leave?

The answer may be that your former partner has drained all your resources, and there's nothing left to take. Or your former partner has simply found a juicier target. Or your partner simply decides that he or she is bored. For whatever reason, you are no longer of any use, and the sociopath is gone.

If this person doesn't return, consider yourself lucky.

The return

Sometimes the sociopath does return. They often have a sixth sense of when you may be receptive to hear from them. They just seem to know when your anger has subsided, or when you're feeling lonely, or when you feel strong enough to be "just friends."

Then, because they've spent so much time studying you, they know exactly what approach to use to hook you again.

They may proclaim their love, confessing that they never knew how much they truly loved you until you were gone.

They may apologize profusely, seeming to take responsibility for their heartless actions, while conveniently blaming something else, such as work stress or alcohol.

They may promise to go to counseling, or church, or rehab. Or, they say they've already been to counseling, church or rehab, and they've changed.

Or, they seduce you sexually.

Why do they return? Perhaps the "juicier target" has thrown them out and they have no place to go. Whatever the reason, they were able to manipulate you before, so they assume they'll be able to manipulate you again.

Maintain No Contact

In numerous articles on Lovefraud, I've explained that to end an involvement with a sociopath, you must have No Contact with him or her.

If the sociopath returns after a period of time, your response should be the same: Maintain No Contact.

They may catch you off-guard by contacting you from a new phone number or email address that you haven't blocked. They may show up unannounced at your home or place of employment.

Do not fall for their apologies, excuses or professions of love.

Never forget: Once they are adults, sociopaths do not change. Sooner or later, the old games will start again, except they'll be worse.

If a sociopath returns, do not let him or her back into your life.

7 classic lies from sociopaths and how to spot them

Sociopaths lie. No matter what type of relationship you have with a sociopath — romantic, family, business or casual — sooner or later the sociopath will lie to you. The circumstances may vary, the scale of the lie may vary, but at some point the sociopath will tell you something that simply isn't true.

Following are seven classic lies from sociopaths (people who could be diagnosed with antisocial, narcissistic, borderline, histrionic or psychopathic personality disorders). How many have you heard?

1. I love you

Sociopaths are incapable of love, as you and I understand it. Real love includes caregiving, and sociopaths simply cannot put someone else's wellbeing before their own. However, they have learned that if they say, "I love you," they get what they want. So they easily mouth the words. Do not believe them.

2. I'll pay you back

Sociopaths often, although not always, ask their targets for money. They'll say that you are the only one who can help them, or offer you a surefire investment opportunity. They'll even sign a contract or promissory note. They'll promise to repay you — but these promises are useless. The only time you'll see your money is when they are trying to establish credibility — so they can ask you for more money later, which will never be returned.

3. You can trust me

Beware of anyone who proclaims that they are trustworthy. Those who feel the need to tell you that they are trustworthy probably aren't. And why are they saying this in the first place? Are you questioning their behavior or requests? If you are, pay attention — your intuition is trying to warn you of danger.

4. I'm not married

For a sociopath, marriage is simply a contract giving them access to their spouse's assets, or control them in some way. Love and fidelity have nothing to do with marriage. So if sociopaths want to have sex with you, or target you for some other reason, well, they ditch their marriage vows like a winter coat on a summer day.

5. I can't get (you) pregnant

Female sociopaths view pregnancy as a meal ticket — if they have your child, you have to pay them for 18 years. Male sociopaths view pregnancy as a control mechanism — once you are pregnant, you are tied to them for 18 years. Therefore, they have no qualms about lying to you about birth control.

6. My phone died

You've been unable to reach the sociopath, possibly for days. You may be sick with worry — has something happened? Then suddenly, he or she answers, as if you just spoke 10 minutes ago. You express your worry, and the answer is a shrug — the phone died. The truth, however, is that the person was with someone else, or intentionally trying to upset you.

7. Everyone thinks you're crazy

This is a double-barreled lie. First of all, there's nothing wrong with you — except, perhaps, the sociopath. Secondly, the sociopath is saying that your friends, family and associates are talking about you, when it's likely that no one is saying a word. The sociopath's objective is to put you on the defensive, and assert control over you.

59

How to know when the sociopath is lying

The problem with lies is that we're not very good at detecting them. In fact, research shows that human beings can spot lies only about 53% of the time. That's little better than flipping a coin.

And all those tips about how spot a liar — like they won't make eye contact, or they'll give themselves away with microexpressions — well, the tips don't work with sociopaths. Remember, these are the people who can beat polygraph tests.

So what can you do?

Sociopaths lie like they breathe. They tell big lies and little lies. They mix lies with the truth, so you don't know what's real and what is not. And they often lie for the fun of it. So if you are sure, or relatively certain, that you're dealing with a sociopath, then you must assume that anything out of his or her mouth is potentially a lie.

But what if you don't realize that you're dealing with a sociopath?

The best thing you can do is trust your intuition. If a statement strikes you as odd or improbable, or if you get a bad feeling about what someone says, pay attention. It could be a warning that the person is lying.

You may have been taught to give people the benefit of the doubt. Recognize that this is extremely risky. If you perceive that something is amiss, don't talk yourself out of your perception.

Your instincts are designed to keep you safe. For your instincts to work, you need to listen to them.

How do you help someone snared by a sociopath?

Lovefraud heard from a woman who was concerned for her daughter. Here is her email:

Currently, our daughter is married to a sociopath. He has taken us (her parents) for thousands and thousands of dollars, then turned her against us. These people victimize people and are somehow able to make themselves look like the victim. They have 2 small children.

He has completely isolated her from her family, including her sister. He completely hates me and has made me the enemy, for I started seeing through him. Do you have any idea how I can possibly reach her to make her see the pattern? This man has felonies on his record for scheming to defraud; he has cheated people all his adult life. I have found out many other disturbing things about his past that she is not aware of. I want to inform her of these things, however many people feel she won't believe it. Like your sociopath, this one said he was in the Gulf War; he never was. Instead he went AWOL from the service. He said he had a masters degree in accounting, but he has no college degree of any sort. He's had over 20 jobs and moved over 30 times. He is 12 years older than our daughter, has a terrible temper. We worry about her and the babies all the time.

What's a mother to do? On the one hand, she sees knows that her daughter's husband is toxic. On the other hand, her daughter is a grown woman making her own decisions.

Sociopathic manipulation

The woman's daughter is being manipulated by a professional. Sociopaths gradually draw in their victims with flattery and half-truths. Then they hold on to their victims with empty promises or threats. Eventually the victims, confused by the alternating charm and rage, are emotionally off balance and doubting their own perceptions.

It happened to me. It happens to everyone snared by a sociopath.

The problem for me was that I didn't know about sociopaths. I had no idea that it was possible for a man who consistently claimed that he loved me, to lie, cheat on me, and take my money. I had no idea such evil existed.

Friends and family

Sociopaths put a lot of energy into maintaining the charade for their victims. They don't put the same energy into manipulating people on the periphery. Consequently, the friends and family of the victim can often see the deception when the victim doesn't.

Friends and family should do their best to maintain a relationship with the victim, but they need to be cautious about trashing the perpetrator. Sociopaths tell the victim that everyone is against them, and criticizing the sociopaths will prove this to be true. But I also think friends and family should not enable the sociopath by continuing to give money or whatever else he is demanding. The sooner the supply ends, the sooner the sociopath will leave.

I suggested that the woman do her best to maintain contact with her daughter, even though the sociopath has isolated her. At some point, he will abandon her. When he does, I recommended that the woman not be judgmental toward her daughter.

I know the devastation of being victimized by a sociopath. Once I realized the truth, what I needed was not criticism, but the support of people who cared about me.

Is it parental alienation,
or protecting children from sociopaths?

The Lovefraud reader "tootrusting" posted the following as a comment on yesterday's article, *Horrifying saga of multiple predators, sexually abused children and murder*. She asked an important question.

> Donna, have you heard about the young 12-year-old girl in Georgia, who took her own life, and streamed it live for all to see? This tragedy occurred December 30, 2016, and I just learned of it yesterday. It seems she had to grow up very young in life, and just could not take it anymore. This story has rocked me, and my heart breaks for the life this young soul endured. It appears many people, whom she should've been able to count on, repeatedly let her down. Mom, Dad, Step-father, etc.
>
> Anyway, in obsessively reading as much as I could about this young girl, I stumbled on a term — Parental Alienation. A reader, who evidently is composing a book on this subject matter, was trying to get into contact with this girl's father, thinking he (and she) were a product of parental alienation. So I got to researching — mainly because I had never heard of parental alienation, and how it affects the children and/or parents involved.
>
> My ex, the father of my child, is a sociopath (or a narcissist — probably both). I reached out to you last May via email to seek some guidance in my own personal situation.

First, thank you for your response. I don't think I said that at the time.

To recap, my ex assaulted me with a gun when I was 26 weeks pregnant with our child. The incident lasted a little more than an hour, and during the entire event, he repeatedly made me think he was going to shoot me. I walked away (obviously), pressed charges, went to court, he lied, got off with a slap on the wrist, etc.

I became a hot hormonal mess after delivering my baby girl — stuff like: my daughter's not going to have a father, poor her, poor me, poor him. I ended up contacting him when she was a month old, and invited him to have a relationship with her.

It lasted all of 6 months or so, during which time, I discovered I suffered from PTSD from the gun saga. So, basically, even if he's not trying to kill me, I become extremely paranoid (in my head) that he is. I'm still not convinced that paranoia inducing wasn't part of his master plan, to screw with my mind. Anyway he's been out of our lives since April of 2013.

October of 2015 I heard from someone in his family, and then started to hear from him on a monthly basis. I never bit. I never responded. I reached out to you when the fear became paralyzing, and you encouraged me to continue my stint of no contact. Which I have. He last reached out to me on Christmas Day, 2016.

Anyway, my point of all this (cuz I do have one) is: am I doing parental alienation? When I had my daughter, I never named him on her birth certificate in an effort to create a roadblock, albeit temporary, once he decides to pursue it. I'm petrified he'll hurt our daughter, or use her to hurt me, try to turn her against her brothers or me, mentally mess her head up — all of the above really.

This whole time I justify not responding to him (which I would like to point out she had three birthdays before he ever reached out to her/me) as I am protecting her, and me, and us. She has asked about him a few times, and I try to keep my answers as short and non-critical of him as possible. Things like yes you do have a dad, no he's not in heaven, I don't know where he is; and then she starts talking of something else.

I still have a big question mark in regards to how to handle answering the tough questions when they come. But — Parental Alienation — are my actions fitting that description? Am I messing her up in my quest to protect her? I don't know that there's a book for dummies on this particular subject. Any help or suggestions are welcomed.

I should also mention he hasn't changed and I sincerely don't think he needs yet another chance. I stumbled on a social media post of a very recent ex girlfriend of his. She described a violent situation that occurred between he and her that mirrors many situations he had with me.

Donna Andersen responds

Tootrusting,

First of all, your ex is likely a violent sociopath, especially if he is exhibiting the same behavior with a recent romantic partner. The best thing you can do is keep him out of your life, and out of your daughter's life. However, you may need to be careful about how you accomplish this, in case he ever decides to claim that you engaged in parental alienation.

The entire concept of parental alienation is a minefield.

Dr. Richard Gardner

The concept of parental alienation was promulgated by a man named Dr. Richard Gardner. As explained by Joan Zorza, J.D., writing in Domestic Violence, Abuse, and Child Custody Legal Strategies and Policy Issues, parental alienation "blames the mothers for any hostility that the children feel towards their fathers, maintaining that children normally always love and respect their fathers unless mothers poison the children against them, even when the fathers beat or sexually abuse the mothers and/or children."

Zorza, and many people who support abused mothers, say that

parental alienation is "junk science." They point out that Gardner's theories have no scientific basis and were never recognized in the mental health profession. Plus, Gardner had other ideas that were downright disturbing. Zorza writes:

> "Gardner also advocated many deviant sexual behaviors, including sexual sadism, child sexual abuse, necrophilia, and sex involving animals, enemas, or urination as supposedly beneficial, normal behaviors."

Many people who advocate for battered women and battered mothers insist that parental alienation does not exist, and that abusive men use the claim to take children away from good and loving mothers.

Sociopathic parents

But just about anyone who has attempted to co-parent with a vindictive sociopath knows that parental alienation does exist. Whether the sociopathic parents are mothers or fathers, they frequently do everything they can to badmouth and denigrate the other parent. The sociopaths' goal is to hurt the other parents where it hurts the most, by prying away their children. Unfortunately, sometimes they succeed.

Furthermore, many parents like you, Tootrusting, have good reason to want to keep their children away from their former partners. The exes may be violent, abusive and negligent. Even when the abuse isn't physical, if the parent is sociopathic, there will likely be psychological or emotional abuse, which is just as damaging to children.

Clueless courts

Unfortunately, most family court officials believe that all children should have two parents. They don't understand that sociopathic parents damage their children, and that children have a better chance of growing up to be healthy if sociopathic parents are not in their lives.

Furthermore, sociopath parents — whether they are the mothers or fathers — are adept at accusing their former partners of parental alienation. They cry in court, plead that they "only want to be in their children's lives," and judges buy it. In many cases, the judges take the children away from non-disordered parents, who are legitimately accusing the other parent of abuse, and award them to the sociopaths.

Incapable of love

So Tootrusting, here is my advice for you:

Understand that sociopaths are not capable of loving anyone, including their children. If your ex is asking for contact with the child, it is likely a pretext to have contact with you, and perhaps draw you into his web again. I recommend that you continue to ignore him as long as possible. Hopefully he will just go away.

Know that no matter what other people say to you, children do not need both of their parents when one of them is a sociopath. Understand that the less contact your daughter has with her father, the better her chances of growing up healthy and happy. Do not feel like you should encourage your daughter to have a relationship with her father.

Keep your case out of court if at all possible. If your ex ever starts ramping up the pressure and threatens that he will take you to court to enforce his parental rights, you may want to agree to let him see the child in a public place. Perhaps you can make arrangements to meet at a Chuck E. Cheese, or someplace like that.

Then, send your daughter with a trusted friend or relative. Do not go yourself. Most likely, he just wants to get his hooks into you again, and that can't happen if you don't show up. If he asks for contact again, do the same thing. Hopefully, after a few times, he will lose interest, and that will be the end of the court threats.

The custody game

But if he does pursue a court case, recognize that you are now involved in a custody game, and you do not want to be accused of parental alienation. So don't say anything bad about him.

You may want to pretend to be willing to allow him to see your daughter, while stalling as long as possible. The older she is before having contact with her father, the more she will be able to protect herself, or at least tell you what happens when she's with him.

In any event, be sure to document everything that happens. Courts want evidence in order to make decisions. If he has a pattern of asking for visits and then not showing up, or if he mistreats your daughter in any way, you want to have a record of it.

Tootrusting, parental alienation takes place when a parent vindictively keeps children away from a healthy parent. Even though he might accuse you of parental alienation, that's not what you are doing. You are legitimately protecting your daughter. But you may need to be careful, because many courts don't understand that.

15 typical crises sociopaths create in our lives, and how to start your recovery

Sociopaths can drain us of everything we've got. By the time many of us understand that we're dealing with a human predator, we look around and realize that we are depleted in many areas of our lives.

Here are 15 typical crises caused by sociopaths:

1. Our money is gone.
2. We are heavily in debt and our credit is gone.
3. Our housing situation is perilous — we are homeless, in danger of becoming homeless, or stuck living with the sociopath.
4. We don't have reliable transportation.
5. We're not working — the sociopath promised to support us, or we're working for the sociopath, or we are so stressed that we can't work.
6. We've been isolated from family and friends.
7. The sociopath has been spreading rumors about us, so our reputation is trashed.
8. We are anxious, depressed or traumatized.
9. We are physically ill from the stress. We've come down with fibromyalgia or some other autoimmune disease, or even cancer.
10. We've contracted a sexually transmitted disease from the sociopath.
11. If we have children with the sociopath, they are also

traumatized, or the sociopath is threatening to take them away.

12. The sociopath has gotten us arrested — probably for something we didn't do.

13. If we're in court, for a divorce or some other claim, the sociopath is lying and pulling out all the stops in order to win the battle.

14. We've lost our faith in God or our higher power.

15. We've lost our faith in ourselves. In fact, we don't recognize ourselves.

Any one of these crises would be bad. But when we're involved with a sociopath, usually we are facing many of them at once. So what do you do? How do you begin to recover?

Two steps forward to start your recovery

I believe you start with two critical steps:

1 . Recognize what you are dealing with

The person is a sociopath — educate yourself about what that means. They are exploiters. Human predators. You've been confused by the lying, demands and attacks — but that's what sociopaths do. He or she is disordered and will not change.

2. Begin to disengage emotionally

The sociopath played on your love, concern and sympathy, in order to control you emotionally. You, as a normal human being, tried to be understanding. But no matter what he or she has told you, it's not your fault. Nothing you could have done would have made the sociopath treat you any better.

No matter what daunting practical matters you face — like leaving, finding a place to live or getting a job — the initial steps to recovery are internal. You need to see clearly what the sociopath is all about, and internalize the fact that you deserve better.

From this mindset, you can begin to rebuild your life.

3 vital concepts about sociopaths
that are key to our survival

Two Lovefraud readers recently sent in articles explaining their views regarding their experiences with sociopaths. Their opinions are almost completely opposite from each other.

In *The importance of recognizing the complexities of sociopath relationships,* the reader "Andrea19" suggests a nuanced way of looking at our experiences with sociopaths. Yes, her ex-husband is manipulative and deceptive, she writes, but she acknowledges that she has her own mental health issues that contributed to the dysfunctional relationship.

The Lovefraud reader "Lanie19" takes a different view. In her article, *I lived among sociopathic monsters all of my life,* she comes out and says, "They are all monsters." Her view is that it doesn't matter if the person is a psychopath, antisocial or narcissist, they are all destructive.

If you haven't read these articles yet, I invite you to do so. They allude to three important concepts that are critical to surviving sociopaths.

Concept #1: Millions of people living among us have serious personality disorders in which they exploit and manipulate the rest of us

We need to know that our world is full of dangerous people, and they don't necessarily look like criminals or drug dealers. These people are fundamentally different from the rest of us, in that they do not follow the rules of civil society. They also do not have the ability to love as the rest of us do.

Lovefraud refers to this category of people collectively as sociopaths, which is consistent with the original meaning of the term. (For more explanation, read the Lovefraud page, *What's a sociopath?*) They are pathological in their social relationships — they intentionally use, abuse, exploit and manipulate almost everyone of significance in their lives.

This is a massive problem. Perhaps 12% of the population are sociopaths — that's 30 million adults in the United States. These disordered individuals are everywhere. They can be found in all segments of society.

Whether we realize it or not, we have probably all run across sociopaths in our lives.

Concept #2: Although all sociopaths intentionally manipulate and take advantage of others, they don't all do it in the same way, to the same extent, or for the same reasons

Lovefraud uses "sociopath" as an umbrella term covering people who would be clinically diagnosed as having antisocial, narcissistic, borderline, histrionic or psychopathic personality disorders. These people all engage in manipulation and exploitation, but there are differences and distinctions among the disorders.

Psychopaths and antisocials are the worst. These are the people with no conscience and no remorse. Some are cold and calculating. Some are capable of violence. Some will target and even destroy others just to entertain themselves.

All psychopaths and antisocials are narcissistic, but not all narcissists are psychopathic or antisocial. Part of the difference is in the degree of malice. Psychopaths and antisocials will intentionally hurt someone, whereas narcissists are so focused on themselves that they don't notice when they hurt people. Professionals have also identified several different varieties of narcissists. Some are blatant. Some are covert. Some think highly of themselves, and some seem to be acting narcissistically in order to cover up deep-seated insecurities.

Histrionics always want to be the center of attention and use people to get what they want. They are often sexually promiscuous.

Those with borderline personality disorder are probably the saddest cases. Women with borderline personality disorder were often sexually abused while young. Men with borderline personality disorder often experienced guilt and shame while young. As a result, they do not have a clear sense of identity.

Unlike psychopaths, antisocials and narcissists, borderlines suffer because of their disorder. But they still engage in manipulative and exploitative behavior with others.

Concept #3: Sociopaths figure out our vulnerabilities and use them against us

Sociopaths are responsible for their vile actions. Through deception and manipulation, they take advantage of us. But how do they do it? By targeting our vulnerabilities.

My intention is not to blame the victim. But the unfortunate truth is that in many cases, we participate in our own victimization. This can happen in many ways. We may be lonely, depressed or anxious, and the sociopath promises to make us feel better. We have goals and dreams, and the sociopath promises to make them come true. Or we get so much satisfaction from helping others that we're willing to give more than we get, to the point that we end up depleted.

This can happen to anyone. Why? Because we all have vulnerabilities.

A vulnerability just means that we want something. The sociopath turns whatever we want into a hook in order to catch us.

Key to surviving sociopaths

Taken together, these three concepts are the key to our survival. If we know that sociopaths exist, that they come in several different varieties, and that they use our vulnerabilities against us, we stand a chance against them. When we feel like we are being manipulated, with this knowledge we can recognize what is happening and escape before too much damage is done.

Forewarned is forearmed.

Exposing the sociopath

Last week Lovefraud received the following email from a reader that brought up an important issue:

> I would like to expose the person who bilked me for thousands of dollars. I am going to file a claim in small claims court so there will be some public record, but I thought about having a web site that would be linked when someone Googled his name. Is this legal? If I tell only the truth about him, is that legal? I want to protect other women from this sociopath; I don't know how. I thought if people were able to Google his name and know about his lies and deceit, they could have the knowledge I never did and could make better choices than me. Any and all information would be helpful.

Many people have asked the same question — can I expose the sociopath? Unfortunately, there is no easy answer. Several different laws apply, and the laws have been interpreted differently by various courts. Here's a brief overview of the situation regarding U.S. law.

Lawsuit for anything

First of all, there are two types of law in the United States: criminal law and civil law.

It is unlikely that you would be arrested, or end up in jail, for exposing the actions of a sociopath. Although in some states libel is on the books as a criminal offense, it is rarely prosecuted.

However, under civil law in the United States, anybody can sue for anything. Whether the person who files a lawsuit actually wins is another issue—it depends on whether it can be proven that an actual law was broken.

But here's what you have to keep in mind: If you expose the sociopath, and the sociopath files a lawsuit against you, you will have to defend yourself whether the lawsuit has merit or not. There's a good chance that you'll have to retain an attorney, which is going to cost you money.

Some sociopaths love to file lawsuits. And, as we've discussed many times here on Lovefraud, they're experts at manipulating the legal system. Therefore, you should ask yourself these questions:

- Is this sociopath prone to filing lawsuits?
- Does the sociopath have the resources to hire an attorney?
- Do you have the resources to defend yourself if the sociopath takes you to court?

Suppose you've considered these questions and you want to move ahead with exposing the sociopath. You'll want to maximize the chances that you'll win a lawsuit if the sociopath files one. For that, you'll need a basic understanding of media law.

Media law

There are two basic types of law to consider when exposing a sociopath. They are:

- Defamation, which includes libel and slander
- Invasion of privacy

Libel is publication of false information that injures a living person's reputation. (Libel refers to statements or pictures that are published. Slander refers to false statements that are spoken.)

75

Invasion of privacy is the publication of information, even if it is true, that is highly offensive to an ordinary person.

We'll take a closer look at both of these types of claims. However, keep in mind that the information presented here is general. Every state in the U.S. has its own libel and invasion of privacy laws—it's best to research what they are.

Libel

In order for a sociopath to proceed with a defamation case, the following must be present:

- Sociopath must be identified
- Statements made must be false
- Statements must be defamatory
- Statements must be published

In many libel cases, the plaintiff has to spend time proving that published statements are defamatory. Some statements, however, are considered defamatory *per se*, which means anyone would understand them to be defamatory. The plaintiff doesn't have to prove the fact that they are defamatory.

Traditionally, defamation *per se* includes:

- Allegations that injure a person's trade, profession or business
- Allegations of sexually transmitted disease or mental illness
- Allegations of "unchastity"
- Allegations of criminal activity

It's highly likely that if you're exposing a sociopath, you'll make these types of allegations. Sociopathic behavior typically includes unsavory business practices, sexually transmitted diseases, promiscuity and criminal activity. So you can count on your statements being considered defamatory.

Therefore, you must make sure that your statements are true, and you can prove it. In most U.S. states, truth is an absolute defense in libel cases.

Opinions are often not considered to be defamatory. However, if an opinion includes a false statement of fact, it can be defamatory.

Some statements are "privileged." This means that even if a statement is defamatory, the person who makes it is excused from liability. Statements made during judicial proceedings in open court have absolute privilege. Anything said in court by anybody—judges, attorneys, plaintiff, defendant, witnesses—can be reported without fear of defamation. This protection is also extended to any legal documents filed with the court.

Invasion of privacy

Publishing private and intimate facts about a person, or information that is highly offensive and is not of legitimate concern to the public, can be considered an invasion of privacy.

Information about the following are generally considered to be protected by the right of privacy:

- Private letters
- Sexual orientation or sexual relations
- A person's health
- A person's wealth

Public records, such as birth, marriage and military records, may be published.

Truth is not a defense in an invasion of privacy case. Again, sociopaths often engage in behavior that reasonable people would consider offensive. Even when statements about the behavior are true, you may not be protected from an invasion of privacy claim.

Invasion of privacy claims are sometimes made because of how information is gathered. If you use surveillance, a hidden camera or a hidden microphone, your actions might be considered intrusion.

Free speech

You might be asking, "What about the First Amendment?"

"What about my right of free speech?"

The First Amendment of the United States protects the freedom of the press and various rights of free speech from government censorship. The First Amendment does make it more difficult for libel cases to be pursued in the U.S. as opposed to other countries. And public figures often have to prove "actual malice" to win a libel case. However, it does not mean anyone can say anything they want about a private individual.

In the past, only journalists and newspapers had to worry about libel and invasion of privacy laws. But with the Internet, anyone can publish anything, and the law has not caught up with the technology. Therefore, there are no clear-cut guidelines about what you can do, and what you can't.

Exposure works

At Lovefraud, I know that exposure works. Four women have contacted me from Australia. They met my ex-husband, James Montgomery, who is still fishing for victims online, but after Googling him and reading my story, ditched him.

The same has happened with other True Lovefraud Stories—I know that people have escaped involvements with Phil Haberman, Lance Larabee, Anthony Owens, Patti Milazzo, Michele Drake, Brian Ellington and Bill Strunk.

Because the legal and judicial system is so inadequate in dealing with sociopaths, in my opinion, exposure is the only thing that does work.

If you want to proceed

Therefore, if you're thinking about exposing the sociopath who victimized you, first you must weigh the risks. Is the sociopath likely to sue? Are you in a position to defend yourself?

If you want to proceed, here are some points to keep in mind:

- Calling the person a "sociopath" may be problematic, unless you can prove an actual diagnosis. Implying a mental disorder is defamation *per se.* You may want to skip the term and just publish what the person did.

- Make sure you can prove that any statement you make about the sociopath is the truth. Stick to the facts.
- Don't make any threats, even facetious threats. Avoid statements like, "Does anybody know a good hit man?"
- You may have more leeway if the sociopath is a public figure. In order to win a libel suit, the sociopath would have to prove "actual malice." For example, if Joey Buttafuoco proceeds with his libel suit against Mary Jo, part of her defense may be to claim he is a public figure.
- If you are currently involved in a legal action with a sociopath, you should probably wait until it is over before publishing anything that might damage your case. The exception to this might be criminal cases in which the prosecutors aren't taking any action. Sometimes media attention gets them to move, as in the Ed Hicks case.
- If you've been to court with the sociopath, you can use anything that was part of the court proceedings— any legal documents filed, anything said in court. Get the transcript, especially if the sociopath lied and you can prove it.
- Public records, such as criminal convictions, can be published.
- If you're building a webpage to expose the sociopath, don't make up a cute title like, "Five years of deception." Use the person's name in the url. That's the best way for the page to show up when someone Googles the name.
- Finally, if you're going to expose the sociopath, make sure you can do it safely. If the sociopath is violent and on the loose, put your own safety before trying to save others.

What if he says he'll get help?

Lovefraud recently received the following email from a woman whom we'll call "Callista." I'll have some comments at the end.

This is yet ANOTHER email from a woman who realized she had been with a sociopath. In my case, it's been for 8 years. He fits the bill on all counts, except that while his finances are always a mess, he met me when I was coming out of a divorce and mine were a mess too. So he didn't see me as a "mark" he could use and swindle.

He is now paying me support and believe it or not he was not only impeccable about paying it to his ex-wife, he is also impeccable about paying me. This confuses me because he lacks the trait of screwing EVERYONE. Don't get me wrong, there is a trail of foreclosures, faulting on bank loans and people he's never paid back.

He moved from me and was immediately living with someone else. Denying it all along. I have done enough reading to know the traits and I know pity is one of their favorites. I have never sat by when I discovered something. I was just never looking. I trusted him. Sigh. He came over and I told him I was saying goodbye and that I would not be speaking, or seeing him again. I told him of what I read and learned about his pathology. He came over angry because he had promised one arrangement and as usual denied he made the deal (even though

80

it was recorded in a text message. "That's not what I meant," he said.) He hates when I hold him accountable, as they all do.

I told him I had been reading about his pathology. Trying to understand him and how my own pathology fits into his. I told him about sociopaths. If you have read as much as you think you have, you know there is a brain connection. He had fallen as a young child, head first into a concrete basement (they had just poured it and removed the stairs). He also had epilepsy as a child and I would bet dollars to donuts, it was in the frontal lobe.

When I explained all the traits, he really looked sad. He once said to me, "I may be a bastard, but it doesn't mean I don't have feelings." As we know, this still only means he has feelings for himself and no other. But he was acknowledging his lack of relationships and admitting to the traits and asked me what he can do about it. I told him that based on what I read there is nothing he can do, but that they can very effectively diagnose him and that the first thing he should do is get an evaluation done. He reached out to me and said, "It's not my fault. You've given me something to think about."

I just left for 3 weeks. The "goodbye" conversation was when he was coming over to pick up the dog. He then said, "let's not talk and give me a chance to read up on this and then when you get back we can talk". And THEN he said, "If I admitted to all the women I was involved with, do you think we could put it all behind us and move forward together?" Here is my thought on that. On the one hand, my own wishful thinking is thinking that perhaps there is a part of him that understands there is an issue. Perhaps he does have a conscience? His perfect record of paying support indicates he has some decency. Or perhaps he knew the EXACT thing and the ONLY thing he could say to me in that parking lot, (as he left for his new girlfriend's apartment), that would stop me from fully disengaging. He used the pity card and he used the intimacy he knows we seem to experience so deeply together.

As you can see, I'm struggling with this. What's real? What's not real? Based on what I have read, I have to conclude that the entire exchange is ENTIRELY false. I know so much of it is, but is it really false to the core? Can he perhaps have a part of him that can prevail and nurture the part of him that does have goodness? He is incredibly kind to our animals. He'd kill anyone who would harm them in ANY way.

Don't get me wrong, this man has done the unthinkable. He has crossed every decent line there is. I know the answer for sociopaths to "can they be saved?" is "no."

Ok down to the question. Did he simply use his cunning ability to do and say the only and exact thing that would stop me from cutting that final thread? Or are there some who are sociopaths to a lesser degree? I know he is weary of all the secrets and lies and the life he leads. I can see it. He just doesn't know how to get out. It's all he's known. I had no idea, until I learned the trail of women from his past and how many he continued to carry on with and keep "on the line" for years and years. So am I just another he's trying to add to the "back burner" in case his latest doesn't work out?

I would NEVER entertain reconnecting with him unless he came to me and said, "I want to get evaluated and I want to come clean to you." Without that, I wouldn't set one foot near him. So what do I do if he DOES say that? My feeling is I wait to see what the evaluation says and how "clean" the "coming clean" truly is. At the end of the day, I'd bet my life he'd never do it. It's too much of a leap from where he has been for so many years. I don't think he is capable, and while I'm spending my time writing this email, he's having a fun-filled night with a new victim who "can't believe how lucky" she is, and thinks she's died and gone to heaven.

And there's the last question. Do I try and warn her? I wish someone had tried with me. I am guessing she won't believe me, but I would say things that would stick in her mind and acknowledge that I can understand why she would not want to believe what I am saying. He's already cheated on her. I think that's the one thing I could say that might make her stop. Although he's SO good at lying, he'd convince her otherwise. But when things turn bad — and they will — perhaps she'll remember what I said and know there is someone she can seek out to relate to.

So all this rambling is so typical of what these people do to our lives, our souls and our minds.

I am an intelligent, attractive, capable, kind woman. While he told me how worthless I was throughout, I managed to save my core and know that I am of value. But guess what? I stopped loving him — I was FREE of him — I didn't even think of him. Then one day I came home from a grueling business trip. I was tired and lonely and he brought the dog home and sat on the sofa we'd sat on for so many years and we just talked. It was such a comfort. And that turned into a very intense hour in bed. He left and I was a mess. He said he felt connected to me and then went on to keep me twisting in the wind.

I knew he was living with someone. I knew the reason he couldn't just spend time with me was because he couldn't figure his way around not being accounted for. I could go on. I started this, wanting to outline a scenario and ask a simple question. I allowed myself to go on, because I think it demonstrates what happens to people like me. Oh, did I mention that the weekend I had hoped we would spend together and he messed me around — I was so desperate to get him to show me he cared that I took a bottle of pills and sent him a text and told him, thinking he'd "come to my rescue" and guess what he did? NOTHING! I would have died if not for stumbling out of my car (I had parked somewhere) and someone thought I was drunk and called the police. He basically left me for dead. Incredible.

Even more incredible is that I would ever speak to him

again. And yet even more confusing is me explaining to him that someone who is healthy does not do what he did in that situation. Someone who is healthy does not lie to someone who almost died and say "I came by to see you" — "I called the police" — "I called the hospital." I knew he had done none of those and I pointed out to him how only a sociopath would do something like this and his answer was "I need help." DAMN HIM! Why couldn't he have just been a jerk and denied it and argued with me. No, he said the only thing that would not allow me to truly disconnect from him. Or does he truly realize how empty he is and is there something worth saving? Ugh. I'm exhausted.

I wrote this for my benefit. I wrote it for the benefit of anyone else who is going through an experience with a sociopath and has one JUST like mine.

I'll let you know what happens. My bet is that he doesn't give me the "material" to work with and I've basically just delayed my road to recovery by 3 weeks, because between now and when I return, I'll be thinking, "what if he comes to me and says he'll get help?" What if he does want to leave all the shallow relationships behind? What if I am really the only person he has ever loved (to the extent he can love)?

I have never allowed someone to abuse me the way he did. I see through people darn fast and I cut them off. But not this guy. This guy has got his hand on my heart and although I thought I was free, I am not. More work to do. More work to do.

Analysis and comments

Callista,

Your email is a superb example of how confusing it can be to be involved with a sociopath. When it's good, it's very good — but there's so much deceit, game-playing and crazy-making. We're torn between wanting the good times to return, wanting to help and wanting wholeness for ourselves.

First, an answer to one of your questions. Yes, it is possible for sociopaths to be not all bad. Sociopathy encompasses a range of behaviors. In fact, Dr. Robert Hare's Psychopathy Checklist-Revised includes 20 traits, and an individual is scored on each separate trait. So it is possible for someone to score high on something like "deceitful and manipulative" and not as high on "poor behavior controls."

It is possible for one sociopath to love animals, while another sociopath tortures them. My ex-husband, James Montgomery, loved animals, and was always bringing home exotic pets. Many sociopaths are corporate executives, and have enough money to pay their bills. Your ex has chosen to pay you support, at least for the moment. Does that mean he is capable of becoming the man that you deserve? Not necessarily.

Something to think about

You told him what you've learned about sociopathy. This, you said was his reaction:

> He reached out to me and said, "It's not my fault. You've given me something to think about."

And then comes your question:

> Did he simply use his cunning ability to do and say the only and exact thing that would stop me from cutting that final thread?

The answer could very well be yes. Sociopaths study their targets, and know exactly how to get the response that they want. Or, he could have had a glimmer of insight into his behavior. Some sociopaths do understand that they're missing something in human interactions.

It is impossible to know what your ex intended. But either way, the relationship is not healthy for you. The best thing to do is look back at his behavior. He cheated on you. You almost committed suicide because of him, and he didn't care. You can never trust this man to be there for you, to be faithful to you. Even if a childhood brain injury caused his condition — which I would doubt — his rehabilitation is not your responsibility.

So why are you having such a hard time cutting the final thread? It's because sociopathic relationships act upon our brains in the same way as an addiction. Sociopaths instinctively know how to manipulate the human bonding process so that we become attached to them, and have a hard time breaking the attachment. For more on this, read the following article, especially the links at the end: *Choose to break your addiction to a sociopath in 2010.*

One of the components of the addiction is sex. Sex causes the release of a brain hormone called oxytocin. This hormone increases our sense of trust and bonding. This is why it's important not to have sex with a sociopath when you're trying to break off the relationship. Sex makes it more difficult for you to leave.

Warn the next victim

Finally, you asked if you should try to warn the next victim. This is a topic of much debate here on Lovefraud. Personally, I feel that if we can do it safely, we should at least try. Your analysis is correct. Maybe she won't believe it now, but when things go bad, she may remember your words.

Callista, you're on the right track. You know the man has a problem. Your attachment to him is an addiction — this is not a moral judgment, just a statement of how the human bonding process works. Regardless of the degree of his pathology, or whether there is a chance for him to improve, for you he is bad news. Leave him in the dust.

Is there any way to deliver a warning that the new conquest will hear?

Editor's note: Lovefraud received the following email from a reader who posts as "FreedomWithNoRing." Donna Andersen responds below.

I am so thankful for your website. There is so much valuable information there to help with understanding how and why one could get locked in and stay with a sociopath.

I was married to an abusive sociopath for 25 years (I met him when I was 12 years old) and finally found the courage to leave 4 years ago. Divorcing and trying to co-parent with a sociopath is a complete nightmare.

My ex was with another woman for 2 years. Eventually they bought a house together. As soon as they moved in together, I knew the facade would crack and true colors would show because he couldn't maintain it 24/7. Sure enough, each time I would see them out somewhere, there were more and more signs that the relationship was taking a toll on her and she was starting to look physically ill and haggard, for lack of a better term. It wasn't long after the last time I saw them that I heard that she had waited until he was out of the country for 2 weeks and moved all of her things out of the house.

I contacted her via a mutual friend to ask if she was ok. Of course it was an odd question coming from the ex-wife, but I knew she had 3 children from a previous marriage and my conscience wouldn't let me sleep until I at least tried to contact her. She emailed me and thanked me for my concern and said her heart was hurting because he had cheated on her, but she was considering a reconciliation. Knowing that, I couldn't say anything else because of the fear that it would go back to the ex and there would be hell to pay. I simply wished her well, told her I was glad she was ok and left her with this, "The average number of times a woman leaves her abuser before it becomes permanent is 7. When something doesn't feel right, there is a reason. Always trust your gut. Most importantly, please know that you are not crazy."

The "crazy" part clicked for her and the floodgates opened. She had experienced plenty of gaslighting and just as he had me, convinced her that she was the crazy one. We exchanged many more emails and she told me that recognition on the gaslighting nixed any chance of a reconciliation. I sent her to your site, and continued to point out sociopath behavior. As it turns out, the ex-girlfriend and I are more alike than different. Of course we are, these people always choose the empath and the "fixer." It's easy to see, once you figure out the pattern.

We have since become friends and I have apologized to her many times as I felt like I should have warned her. The conclusion that we came to was that even if I had tried, she probably wouldn't have believed me and the information would likely have gone back to the ex-husband. Her words to me, "But he was soooo NICE to me at the beginning." They always are nice at the beginning because they need to tie you to them with a thousand strings.

My question to you is whether you think that is accurate? Is there any chance of the latest conquest of sociopaths hearing a warning of things to come? I couldn't have given the ex-girlfriend the warning because of the consequences to me if the information went back to the ex. Is it a moot point or do you think there is any way to successfully deliver a warning message to women that they will actually hear in these situations or do they have to figure it out on their own?

My other question is how do we start to get this message to young women or even young girls to watch out for sociopath behavior BEFORE they get caught in the trap? My motivation is that if I can prevent even one woman from getting into a relationship with a sociopath or help one woman understand afterward that she was duped and it wasn't her fault because the game was rigged against her from the beginning, that would make my 25+ years of the mindf*ck (sorry, but that word is the perfect description) games and living in hell worth it.

Donna Andersen responds

FreedomWithNoRing I am so glad that you escaped, and glad that you were able to help your ex's next target escape.

About your first question — is there any chance of the latest conquest of sociopaths hearing a warning of things to come? The short answer is that it depends on the individual and the circumstances.

If your ex's next target says she wouldn't have listened to you, then I am sure that is the case. Here is why it is so difficult for people to hear warnings about sociopaths:

1. Society's lack of awareness about sociopaths

Most people do not understand what a sociopath or psychopath is. Even worse, those who think they know what a sociopath or psychopath is are often wrong.

Those who have any awareness about personality disorders may believe that sociopaths and psychopaths are all criminals or serial killers. So if you try to tell someone that his or her new love interest is a sociopath, and that person hasn't done time in jail or murdered anyone, you sound like nothing more than a spiteful ex.

Even if you try to avoid this pitfall by not referring to the person as a sociopath and psychopath, you face another problem. Our society doesn't have an awareness that evil exists. Most of us don't know that people can appear to be loving, caring, human beings, but it's all an act, designed to get past our defenses so we can be exploited.

People who are unaware that human predators live among us will have difficulty believing that their new partner, who appears to be so loving, is actually dangerous.

2. The sociopath has primed the next target not to believe you

Do you remember how your ex described his or her romantic partners before you? Most likely the description was negative — that person was abusive, overbearing, cold-hearted, demanding, unstable, mentally ill, delusional, etc., etc.

Well, that's how your ex is now describing you.

When sociopaths trash their previous romantic partners, they are really, really convincing. Everything was your fault. The sociopath did the best he or she could, but there was no pleasing you. You were a gold digger, cheater, or some other nasty person.

The new partner is appalled at how badly you supposedly treated the sociopath. The new partner already dislikes you, perhaps even hates you, even though you've never met. So is this person going to be receptive to a message from you? Not likely.

3. In the beginning, the new partner is being love bombed

Whether the relationship is new, or they have been together for awhile, if the sociopath hasn't yet sealed the deal and convinced the target to commit, the seduction may still be ongoing.

That means the sociopath is still love bombing — showering the target with attention and affection. And who doesn't like being put on a pedestal? If someone is saying, "I love you," who doesn't want to believe it?

So while the sociopath is promising a lifetime of happily-ever-after, is the new target going to want to give up the dream and believe you? Probably not.

Now, if it's later in the involvement, and the new target has already begun to experience the dark side of the sociopath — well, then he or she may be more willing to listen.

What should you do? If you can warn safely, try

In my personal opinion, if you can warn safely, you should at least try.

The key here is IF YOU CAN WARN SAFELY.

Your first responsibility is to yourself. You need to protect your finances, your livelihood, your court case, your children and your recovery. If your situation will be jeopardized in any way by saying something to the new target, don't do it.

FreedomWithNoRing, this is what you faced. You wrote, "I couldn't say anything else because of the fear that it would go back to the ex and there would be hell to pay." Therefore, you were correct to back off.

But it turned out that you said just enough. You gave the new target just enough validation to trust her own perceptions and get out.

Accept the new target's reaction

If you take the step to warn the new target, one of three things will happen:

1. The target will believe you and get out.
2. The target will not believe you and stay.
3. The target won't believe you right away, but will remember your warning later and get out.

You need to be able to accept whatever happens.

If you're able to help the target escape, that's terrific. If the person doesn't heed your warning, you need to be satisfied with the fact that at least you tried.

Maybe you'll hear at some later time that the person escaped, and maybe your warning will have been partly responsible. But you can't wait for that. You need to move on with your life.

Why I suggest warning the new target

Many other people, including many Lovefraud readers, say no

one should try to warn the new target. They say the person will not listen. You will be wasting your time and emotional energy.

Maybe. And maybe not.

Here's why I think it's important to at least try: Not only could you possibly help the new target, but you could help address the first problem I wrote about — society's lack of awareness about sociopaths.

As a culture, we don't talk about sociopaths — what they are, how they exploit us. And this lack of discussion, this black hole of ignorance, is what enables sociopaths to keep finding new victims.

The fact that predators live among us is the biggest skeleton in the closet of the human race. It's time to open the door and let light shine on the sociopaths.

How to get the message to young people

FreedomWithNoRing, your second question was, "How do we start to get this message to young women or even young girls to watch out for sociopath behavior BEFORE they get caught in the trap?"

The answer is what I just said — we need to start talking about the problem.

I recommend that you and all Lovefraud readers educate yourself about sociopaths. Yes, you've learned about them the hard way. But really research the topic. Learn the traits. Learn the warning signs.

I encourage everyone to understand the disorder enough that you can talk about it in a calm, informed way. And then, when an opportunity arises, go ahead and talk about it in an age-appropriate manner.

That's how we warn people — one conversation at a time.

When the parents of your sociopathic ex want to see their grandchildren

Lovefraud recently received an email from a reader who has a daughter with a sociopath and wants to know what she should do about the sociopath's parents, her daughter's paternal grandparents. She wrote:

> My issue with my daughter's paternal grandparents is that I don't trust them with my daughter. It's not because they are bad people, but because my sociopathic ex has victimized his parents over and over and over again and has no respect for what they say. His mother is his biggest enabler and both of his parents want him to be involved with our daughter (he has abandoned her) in the worst way. They pressure him about it nonstop. I fear that if I allow my daughter to be without me in their care (which is what they are gunning for right now) that they will invite my ex over, and I don't trust what he will do. I'm scared he'll take off with her (only to hurt me, not because he wants to spend time with her) or that he'll begin to damage her emotionally. His parents won't stop him because they don't know how. He controls them and I truly believe they are scared of him.

Here's the short answer: Your primary objective is to limit your daughter's exposure to both her father and his family as much as you can. No Contact would be best.

To look at this further, I'll describe three scenarios involving a sociopath's family.

1. The family is also sociopathic

Sociopathy is highly genetic. Therefore, if your ex is a sociopath, it means that one of his parents is disordered, or there is disorder somewhere on the family tree.

If the parents are disordered, they, like your ex, are incapable of love. They are incapable of being genuinely concerned about your daughter's wellbeing.

So why would they want to see their granddaughter? Because, just like the sociopath, they view her as a possession. They want what they perceive belongs to them.

Therefore, they view access to your daughter as a battle that they want to win. If they have money, they may keep fighting until they win.

If your daughter were alone with them, it's possible that the visits would be okay. Or, she might be neglected, abused or even kidnapped. And yes, I do know of sociopathic grandmothers who have kidnapped their grandchildren.

2. Family members are engaged in wishful thinking

Some families aren't disordered themselves, but know that there is something wrong with their offspring. This is certainly possible, because genetics is a crapshoot. The genes related to personality disorders can be passed on, even if a few generations have gone by without anyone actually exhibiting the traits.

The family may hope that if their son would just spend time with his daughter, it would awaken paternal feelings of love and he would become a normal man. So even if the family just wants a relationship with their grandchild, they may also want their son to have a relationship with the girl, and encourage him to come around when they have the girl.

And yes, you should be concerned about your daughter being damaged by her father. Sociopaths are not capable of love, even for their own children.

3. Family members are pawns

Sociopaths routinely exploit everyone they know, including their parents and families.

In some cases, parents may not really know what the sociopaths are like — especially when the sociopath seems to have a successful career. The sociopaths may lie to their parents about their former partners. The parents believe the lies, and do what they can to help, not understanding the sociopath's true, destructive agenda.

Some parents know the sociopaths are trouble, but they are enablers. The parents keep giving the sociopaths money, subsidizing living arrangements, even bailing them out of jail.

Parents may do this out of guilt, fear, or love — it's really, really hard to turn your back on your child, even when you know that the child is disordered and is not going to change.

Keep the sociopath's family out of your life

The safest thing for you to do is have No Contact with your sociopathic ex and his family. Even when the grandparents mean well, it increases the exposure of you and your daughter to the sociopathic father.

In your case, your ex has abandoned your daughter. The only reason to allow the grandparents to see her is if it is ordered by the court. Some states do have laws designed to enable grandparents to see their grandchildren. Look online to find out the grandparents' rights laws in your state.

If the grandparents really understood their son's disorder, and really wanted what was best for your daughter, they would know that the healthiest thing for her would be for them to stay out of her life.

Why we need to talk about our experiences with sociopaths

Most of us at Lovefraud are here because we've been conned, duped, deceived and betrayed by a sociopath.

Once we finally figure out what we are dealing with, many of us do not tell other people what really happened. After all, it's embarrassing to admit that no, we didn't see it coming, and yes, we fell for the scam. And if we do venture to describe the sociopath's true behavior, we may be met by disbelief. "What? That charming person couldn't possibly have done that. You must have misinterpreted."

We quickly learn that people do not understand what we are talking about. Either they don't believe us, or ostracize us. So we stop talking. We try to hide what happened, even from ourselves.

Our silence on being betrayed by sociopaths has two effects:

1. Our pain is bottled up within us, impeding our own recovery
2. The world does not learn just how many social predators are living in our midst

Talking about it

After my appearance on *ABC 20/20*, I received an email from a Lovefraud reader who wrote:

> I watched the show last night and somehow it unleashed several hidden emotions and feelings which I tried

to bury regarding my situation. My healing has begun slowly month by month and I am now learning how not to be so hard on myself and be more cautious with my future relationships...

This reader experienced a release because someone else who was targeted told her story.

Katherine Underwood suffered tremendously at the hands of Budimir Drakulic, who took more than $410,000 from her. I know for a fact that it was very difficult for Katherine to do the TV show. Anyone who watched could see that she became emotional on several occasions.

Still, Katherine did it. And sharing her story likely helped thousands of other people.

When we talk about our experience, when we stand up and say, "yes, this happened to me," it helps other people who have been targeted realize that they are not alone. This can go a long way towards recovery.

Our own healing

Talking about our experience also helps our own healing. When we share what happened, we are no longer carrying the burden of our pain all by ourselves.

A big reason why it's often so difficult to recover from the devastation of the sociopath is that we feel so isolated, like no one really understands what we experienced.

Unfortunately, often our perception on this is correct. People do not understand what happened. That's why a community like Lovefraud is so important — everyone who reads and posts here does understand.

To know that someone truly empathizes with us is extremely validating. Especially when a sociopath has been calling us "crazy" and "mentally unbalanced," validation can be truly helpful to our recovery.

Breaking the silence

When we discover that we've been duped by a sociopath,

among the multitude of unpleasant emotions we feel are shame and embarrassment. Talking about what happened increases our shame and embarrassment, so we don't do it.

Our silence, unfortunately, benefits the particular sociopath we were involved with, along with all the other sociopaths who prowl the planet. Because we don't talk, society doesn't know they exist, and they continue to get away with their manipulation and deceit.

Yes, sociopaths are in our midst. Sometimes they look scary, but usually they don't — they seem to be just like the rest of us, at least at first. They're attentive and charming. They appear to be our best friend, or a pillar of the community.

Even a guy named Budimir Drakulic, the man who conned Katherine Underwood, was able to pass himself off as trustworthy.

Back in 1994, when Katherine met Drakulic, there was even less awareness of sociopaths than there is now. Today, if nothing else, all of us at Lovefraud at least know that they exist.

Spreading the word

Let's spread the word.

Talking about sociopaths can accomplish three things:

1. Helping someone else recognize that they're involved with a predator
2. Helping our own recovery by sharing the burden of our experience
3. Warning the rest of the world about the predators who live among us

We should educate ourselves about this personality disorder, and when the opportunity arises, talk about it. It may not always be safe to talk about our personal situation. But we can share general information. We can send someone a link to Lovefraud.

Knowledge is power. The first step in protecting ourselves from sociopaths is knowing that they exist.

The massive costs of sociopaths to society

My local newspaper is the Press of Atlantic City. It's a small-town newspaper covering the Atlantic City, New Jersey area. It's not the New York Daily News, the Daily Mail or another British tabloid. Yet as I read the paper one day last week, I was shocked to see one story after another that seemed to illustrate sociopathic behavior.

I shouldn't have been surprised. In my opinion, when adults freely commit crime, aggression, fraud, exploitation, violence, bullying, retaliation or pathological lying, they likely have sociopathic traits.

There is research to back this up, which I'll get to soon. But first, here's the news for July 9, 2014. (Although I saw all of the stories — local, regional and national — in the Press of Atlantic City, in some cases I looked for better versions on other websites to post here on Lovefraud.)

Women may have swindled 45 elderly clients

Barbara Lieberman, an attorney from Northfield, New Jersey, who specialized in elder law, and Jan Van Holt, who ran an in-home senior service, were arrested in March and charged with stealing more than $2.4 million from victims who were in their 80s and 90s. All but one are now dead, and most had no family. Now, at least 10 more victims have been identified, and there may be an additional 25 victims.

Elder-fraud case may yield more victims, AG says on Pres-sofAtlanticCity.com

Woman's home was site of serial killings

Catrina McGhaw rents a house in Ferguson, Missouri, that was once the home of Maury Troy Travis. Travis committed suicide in jail in 2002 after being charged with killing two St. Louis area women. Police suspected him in as many as 20 murders.

McGhaw learned that she was living in the home of a suspected serial killer when she saw her house on television, in an A&E documentary. Some victims had been tied to a pole in her basement.

McGhaw called her landlady, who turned out to be the killer's mother, begging to get out of the lease. The landlady refused. However, the St. Louis Housing Authority said McGhaw can break her lease.

Woman renting suspected serial killer's home to move out early on CBSNews.com

Scandal at the Veteran's Administration

A federal investigative agency is examining 67 complaints of retaliation filed by whistleblowers who reported wrongdoing at Veterans Affairs hospitals and facilities.

A report charged that the medical inspector's office, which was supposed to investigate complaints, instead downplayed them. The medical inspector hotline was suspended, with complaints referred to the VA's Office of Inspector General.

Federal agency examines retaliation claims by VA employees who filed whistleblower complaints, on TimesFreePress.com

Woman didn't want kids, so she killed them

Megan Huntsman, 39, of Pleasant Grove, Utah, strangled or suffocated six infants between 1996 and 2006. She said she was heavily addicted to meth and did not want the responsibility of caring for her babies.

Huntsman packed the tiny bodies in separate boxes in her garage. Investigators found a seventh baby that appeared to be stillborn.

Huntsman is in jail, charged with six counts of murder. Bail was set at $6 million.

Mom accused of killing babies while on drugs on PressofAtlanticCity.com

Matthew Sandusky reveals abuse by his father

Oprah Winfrey will interview Matt Sandusky, one of six adopted children of Jerry and Dottie Sandusky, on July 17 at 9 p.m., on the Oprah Winfrey Network.

OWN announced that in the interview, Matt Sandusky describes grooming, methodical control and manipulation by his father, and says he was sexually abused starting at age 10.

Oprah interviews Sandusky son about sexual abuse, on PhillyMag.com

New Jersey man scams investors

Peter Lareau of Mountain Lakes, New Jersey, admitted that he fraudulently obtained $500,000 in an investment scheme. He claimed to be funding educational television programming for teenagers and promised favorable returns to investors.

Instead, he used the money for personal expenses including groceries, tuition payments for his child, rent and club memberships.

Man pleads guilty in fraudulent investment scheme on APP.com

Pithy observations by a news columnist

This wasn't a news story, but a column by Richard Cohen. In it, he imagines that Michael Corleone of The Godfather announces to his henchmen that the mob family is going to incorporate. They would be listed on the stock exchange "with the other criminals." Why? Because when corporations commit crimes, they pay a fine, but no one ever goes to jail.

On Wall Street, the Corleone family fits right in on Washing-tonPost.com

The cost of crime

How much does crime cost U.S. society? A researcher by the name of David A. Anderson came up with a figure of $2.3 trillion per year in 2009 dollars.

In this figure, Anderson included direct costs such as lost property, and indirect costs such as police, courts, prosecutors, public defenders, jurors and prisons. Anderson noted that $2.3 trillion per year was the same amount of money that the U.S. spent on all life insurance policies, all mortgage debt, and all health expenditures.

And who is committing this crime?

Researchers Kent A. Kiehl, Ph.D., and Morris B. Hoffman, figured out how much U.S. crime can be attributed to psychopaths. In a paper called *The Criminal Psychopath: History, Neuroscience, Treatment and Economics*, they point out that between 15% and 25% of males in North American prisons are psychopaths.

Then, assuming an average figure of 20% to do the math, Kiehl and Hoffman calculated that "psychopaths alone are responsible for approximately $460 billion per year in criminal social costs."

How does this compare with other annual societal costs? Take a look:

- $460 billion crime committed by psychopaths
- $329 billion alcohol and substance abuse
- $200 billion obesity
- $172 billion smoking
- $76 billion schizophrenia

Low estimate

This figure of $460 billion per year doesn't even begin to cover the real costs that disordered personalities exact on our society.

Here are reasons why the estimate is low:

1. Kiehl and Morris estimate that 1% of the population are psychopaths, as defined by the Psychopathy Checklist Revised. The American Psychiatric Association, however, estimates that 4% of the population meets the definition of antisocial personality disorder, which is somewhat broader. Plenty of antisocials are also committing crimes. (For more on the differences in terminology, read *Psychopath/Sociopath* on Lovefraud.)
2. Kiehl and Morris did not include women.
3. The estimate does not include civil lawsuits. Sociopaths love to file lawsuits. And if we take sociopaths to court, they do everything the can to run up legal fees, and then do not follow any court orders.
4. The estimate does not include difficult-to-quantify damage suffered by the victims of sociopaths, such as emotional suffering, compromised health, lost jobs and ruined careers.
5. The estimate does not address the costs of having children with a sociopath, such as child custody battles and psychological treatment.
6. The estimate does not address the costs of corporate psychopaths. These are the people who play games with major companies until they collapse, like Enron. One researcher attributed the global financial collapse that began in 2008 to psychopaths in the financial industry.

Root of all evil

I don't think it's an exaggeration to say that sociopaths are the root of all evil in our society, when evil is defined as profound immorality.

Sociopaths are the people who are committing the crimes. They are causing almost all suffering that is not the result of a natural disaster. They may even be the cause of much illness in the world, because of the emotional distress they inflict on their victims.

Yet despite the massive cost that sociopaths inflict on society, most people don't know they exist.

This is why learning about sociopaths is so important. Just knowing that they're out there, and must be avoided, could be the first step in creating a far better world.

How psychopathic parents affect children

A Lovefraud reader who posts as "Mani" asked a question that I'm sure is of interest to many others, so I'll address it in a blog post. Mani writes:

> I was one of the children who lived with a psychopath for a long time. I fought all my life not to let him become a part of my personality. In comparison to what I was exposed to, I think I have been successful. But is there anybody out there who can shed more light on the effects of a psychopath father on children, particularly boys?
>
> I know there is tendency to label these children as secondary psychopaths but I haven't seen anybody talking about the mechanics of it. And I am sure all these children don't become secondary psychopaths.

This is a complex situation with many variables, depending on the individuals involved. I will describe in general terms the two basic types of outcomes. Dr. Liane Leedom has written many articles on the topic. You may also want to get her book, *Just Like His Father?*

By the way, the term "secondary psychopaths" doesn't apply to children of psychopaths. It refers to which set of psychopathic traits are predominant in an individual.

Genetic risk

Psychopathic parents, both fathers and mothers, definitely affect their children in many ways. There are probably two general categories of effects, depending on whether or not the child has inherited a predisposition to become psychopathic.

Psychopathy is highly genetic. That means a child can be born with a predisposition for the disorder to develop. Genetics, of course, is a crapshoot, so a child may or may not get the genes. In fact, a child is more likely to inherit the genes when the mother is psychopathic, rather than the father.

However, psychopathy results from both nature and nurture. Whether this disorder actually does develop is due to the parenting a child receives and the environment that the child grows up in. It is possible, with extremely attentive parenting, to prevent psychopathy from developing, or at least mitigate it. Essentially, parents must teach the child love, empathy and impulse control.

Psychopaths make terrible parents. They will not bother to instill love, empathy and impulse control in a child. They can't teach what they don't know.

Abuse

Psychopathic parents do not love their children. They are not concerned about children growing up to be healthy, productive members of society. They look at children as possessions, like a car or a flat-screen TV.

Some psychopaths neglect their children. Others engage in physical abuse and sexual molestation.

But even if psychopaths don't engage in outright physical abuse, they usually inflict psychological and emotional abuse. They lie to kids, break their promises, and keep changing the rules. The parent may say something, and then insist the words were never spoken, which distorts a child's sense of reality.

The net result is that a child grows up in a very unstable environment. If the child has inherited the genes for psychopathy, chances are good that he or she will develop the disorder. If the child has not inherited the genes, he or she may develop other psychological issues, such as anxiety and depression.

Children of psychopathic parents who are not themselves disordered often have much to overcome related to their families of origin. They may not know what a healthy relationship or a healthy family looks like. They may become involved with sociopaths themselves, because it feels normal.

I think people who have grown up in these situations have a lot of internal untangling to do. They likely need to address and heal deep emotional pain, either through formal counseling or through self-help.

12 rules for negotiating with a psychopath

Lovefraud recently received the following question via email from a reader:

> I have woken up to the fact that I am living among a nest of snakes. This includes my kids that I love. Can you recommend anything to read that helps with negotiating with a psychopath? They are so angry and so nasty. However, things "must" be worked out. Any suggestions on reading materials?

The safest approach to take with a psychopath is not to negotiate at all, to get the person out of your life. Unfortunately, this is not always possible, especially when the psychopath is your spouse and you share children.

So if you do have to negotiate with a psychopath, here are rules to keep in mind:

1. Know your bottom line. Know what you absolutely must have, and know what you can part with. However, do not communicate this to the psychopath. In fact, you should be cautious about communicating it to anyone — you don't want the information getting back to your adversary. And make no mistake — this person is an adversary.

2. The psychopath's objective is to win. Figure out what it is that he/she wants to win. Can you part with it? If so, let it go, although you can pretend to put up a fight just so the psychopath believes he/she has won a big battle.

3. Use an intermediary, such as an attorney. The less personal contact you have with the psychopath, the better. He/she wants to torment you. Don't give the psychopath the satisfaction of doing this.

4. Psychopaths love drama. He/she wants to get a reaction out of you. Do not react. Do not let the psychopath know that you are hurt, angry or upset. Be a rock in the presence of the psychopath — cry when you get home.

5. Do not expect a psychopath to do something because it is right. Do not expect them to be concerned about anyone's wellbeing, including yours or their children's. If they express concern, it's a ploy.

6. Do not be nice. Do not expect the psychopath to be fair. Play hardball.

7. Psychopaths will only act in their own self-interest. Figure out a way to use this against them. What is in his or her self-interest?

8. Psychopaths will lie and manipulate. If you need evidence and documentation, make sure you have it.

9. Psychopaths will seek information from your family and friends, often under the guise of "being concerned." Although your family and friends may mean well, they may fall for the act. Keep your plans to yourself so that they can't reveal anything critical.

10. Any agreement, such as a child custody order, must be detailed, precise and ironclad. If there is one inch of wiggle room anywhere, a psychopath will take a mile. Do not leave any gray areas or ambiguity.

11. Even if you get an agreement, do not expect the psychopath to abide by it — or court orders — willingly. There must be firm deadlines and consequences. Enforce them.

12.Psychopaths only understand power. What power do you hold? Use it.

Do you feel like you're living in a Dr. Jekyll and Mr. Hyde situation? Like the charming, considerate person you thought you were involved with has been replaced by a monster? Know that the charmer was an act, and you are now seeing the real person.

Even though you're probably shocked by the change, you need to understand the mindset that you are dealing with. A book that will help you, which was previously reviewed by a member of Lovefraud, is *The 48 Laws of Power*.

As our reviewer said about the book, "disturbing, but necessary reading."

An open letter to lawyers who have clients involved with sociopaths

Dear Mr. or Ms. Esquire,

When a client tells you his or her opponent is a sociopath, please be aware of the ramifications for your legal case.

First of all, do not disregard the statement just because the opponent hasn't killed anyone. A common perception is that sociopaths are all deranged serial killers. This is not true — only a small percentage of sociopaths commit murder. But all sociopaths are social predators, and live by exploiting others.

Frequently this is financial exploitation — many sociopaths are skilled con artists — but not always. Sociopaths also target people who can provide them with a place to live, business connections, sex, housekeeping or other support services, children, or a respectable image in the community while they live double lives. The point is that sociopaths intentionally use manipulation and deceit to hook their target. They continue the manipulation and deceit to keep the exploitation going, bleeding the target until there is nothing left. At that point, some sociopaths abandon the target, moving on without a backward glance.

Sometimes, however, the target gets wise to the sociopath, and wants to end the involvement. At this point, some sociopaths become enraged at the possibility of losing control, and set out to crush the target. They are not interested in compromise or equitable distribution. They do not want to give the target whatever he or she is entitled to. They want to grind the target into the dirt.

What you need to understand about sociopaths

1. A sociopath's prime objective is power and control. All they want is to win.

2. Sociopaths love the drama of court because it gives them an opportunity to win. They do not consider the possibility that they may lose. If they do lose, they view it a bump in the road, and figure out how to attack the target again. Forcing the target to incur steadily mounting legal expenses is considered a win.

3. Sociopaths lie. They lie convincingly. They have no qualms about lying in court documents or on the witness stand.

4. Sociopaths manipulate other people to lie for them. These witnesses may not know they are lying — they may simply believe everything that the sociopath has told them, because sociopaths are so convincing.

5. Sociopaths feel no obligation to follow court orders or the law. They only follow court orders or the law if they perceive an advantage in doing so. But they are experts at figuring out ways to use the law to further their objective, which is to crush your client.

How people become targets

Most of us believe that people are basically good inside and everybody just wants to be loved. Because we do not know that there are exceptions to these beliefs — namely, sociopaths — we have huge blind spots that these predators can exploit.

No normal person intentionally becomes involved with a lying, manipulative sociopath. So when your client tells you outrageous stories of the sociopath's behavior, and also says he or she never knew about the behavior, or accepted the sociopath's explanations, your client is most likely telling the truth.

How do these entanglements happen? Sociopaths are always on the lookout for people they can use. When they encounter someone through any social interaction, they quickly evaluate whether that person has something that they want. If the answer is yes, they assess the person for vulnerabilities. Then they figure out how to exploit the person's vulnerabilities to achieve their objective.

Sociopaths engage in calculated seduction. If you're handling a divorce case, the seduction was romantic. If it's some other type of case, the seduction may have involved shared beliefs, aspirations or goals. Either way, in the beginning of the involvement, the target is subject to a wonderful honeymoon of admiration and promise.

Once the target is hooked, the sociopath begins the exploitation, while simultaneously ramping up manipulation to keep the target under control. This may involve:

- Isolating the target from his or her support network
- Emotional, psychological, verbal, physical, sexual or financial abuse
- Gaslighting — making the target doubt his or her own perceptions

What you need to understand about the target

1. Involvement with a sociopath is like living in a black hole of chaos. Your client, the target, has probably had every aspect of his or her life disrupted:

- Career interrupted
- Finances ruined
- Health compromised
- Home and property neglected
- Relationships shattered

By the time the legal action commenced, your client may have already been in free fall for a long time. He or she may feel overwhelmed by the magnitude of the issues that need to be addressed.

2. Involvement with a sociopath can cause post-traumatic stress disorder (PTSD). At one time PTSD was diagnosed only in relation to a single traumatic event that involved risk of serious injury or death, coupled with intense fear, horror or helplessness. A new definition identifies a type of PTSD that results from cumulative trauma and long-term injury.

3. PTSD is a psychiatric injury (not a mental illness). PTSD causes biochemical changes in the brain and affects certain areas of the brain's anatomy. Common symptoms include intrusive thoughts, nightmares, flashbacks, difficulty concentrating and exhaustion.

4. The litigation against the sociopath makes your client re-experience the underlying trauma and triggers the symptoms of

PTSD. Dr. Karin Huffer, in her book, *Unlocking Justice,* explains what happens:

> Mentally reliving the trauma during legal proceedings simultaneously activates parts of the brain that support intense emotions while diminishing the functions of the central nervous system that controls motor output, regulates physiological arousal, and impedes the ability to communicate in words. Memory fails and intrusive emotions sabotage concentration on the task at hand. Litigants feel incapable of the spontaneous verbal response and interaction required in typical courtroom exchanges. As a result, the litigant with PTSD might be driven to avoid topics. They literally do not hear them. They disconnect when they need to engage. And, at times, they clearly are nonfunctional and are unable to communicate their symptoms and needs in a formal manner accepted by the courts.

5. Targets of sociopaths have been deceived, betrayed and perhaps subjected to violence. They approach the courts expecting justice, which sociopaths actively thwart. When justice is denied, and targets instead experience profound and prolonged injustice, their PTSD takes on another dimension, which Huffer identifies as "Legal Abuse Syndrome."

Your client's experience

The goal of this letter, Mr. or Ms. Esquire, is to help you understand what your client has experienced. My objective is to explain why he or she may be having difficulties with the litigation process, and difficulties moving on in life. The sociopath intentionally used your client—perhaps for years—and may be intentionally attempting to destroy him or her now.

Your client is not irrational, lazy or obstinate. Your client is having a normal reaction to profound betrayal.

Sincerely,
Donna Andersen
Author, Lovefraud, and a former litigant against a sociopath

Sociopaths and their smear campaigns

Lovefraud received the following letter from a woman who was married to a sociopath for 16 years.

I was a stay-at-home mom until my son entered kindergarten, then I got a job. This was the end of any peace I would have for 10 years. The worst possible thing happened to my husband — the woman he could make fun of for being stupid or having no goals (whatever he would say to hurt my self-esteem) became a huge success. In fact, I made three times as much as Mr. Wonderful. The abuse escalated. He was so obsessed with destroying me that even on a business trip where I was getting an award for being the top sales rep in my company, he was pulling my boss aside and insinuating I was committing fraud and that was why I was #1.

For the last year of my marriage, he had convinced me to hand over all extra money so he could invest for "our" future. I did it thinking it was his ego that was hurt from my success. I didn't know what he was then.

He spent a year hiding every dime, transferring every debt into my name, making up horrible stories about me to my friends and family. He would go talk to them in tears and say I was stealing all of our money and cheating on him. He would say how much he loved me and ask for advice, then have them swear not to say anything to me because he wanted our marriage to work. He even went so far to pull cousins, aunts and uncles aside during my grandmother's funeral to say these things.

At the end of the year, while I was packing for a very large business meeting that was to announce a promotion for me, he told me he had cancer.

I believed him. Who besides a sociopath would say such a lie to their wife? That whole evening was spent crying and upset that my husband had cancer. Then I asked him a simple question, "Who is your doctor?" He couldn't answer. Who would forget their cancer doctor? Then I realized, if he had been going to the doctor for such a serious illness, where were all the insurance bills? I have been to the doctor for a cold and gotten a bill from a lab, the doctor, then a follow-up from the insurance company to pay more, etc. I kicked him out.

I went to my business meeting and the onslaught of horrible screaming calls to the receptionist began from him. An entire week of this, while I was supposed to be there receiving a promotion. I left without the promotion and was basically fired — "maybe you need to take some time to attend to personal problems."

When I came home, I filed for divorce, cried for weeks and then looked around to find our money to pay bills. It was hidden; not a trace of paperwork was left. Every bill was in my name only. My friends, my family, my neighbors, even customers, no longer spoke to me. I deserved this, in their eyes.

Three years later, I still have nobody who fully believes me. I have one friend. My parents and I speak, but I don't trust them not talk to my husband. If he has any information on me, he does whatever he can to destroy me. He abandoned our son, moved to another state to live with the next victim. My own sister sends him cards and letters and won't speak to me.

The smear campaign

This woman was subjected to a smear campaign from her husband, the sociopath.

Abusers often use this tactic to cover up their own behavior and convince others that they are the ones being victimized. In fact, abusers frequently start the campaign as a pre-emptive strike, long before the relationship with the true victim collapses.

That's what happened to the woman who wrote the letter. As the sociopath was getting ready to move on—he probably had his next victim already lined up—he laid the groundwork to destroy his wife. With his tears and skill as a liar, he convinced the woman's friends and family of his story. They became unwitting co-conspirators.

What can you do?

Fighting the smear campaign is difficult. Most honest people can't imagine that someone would be lying when making the outrageous charges that the sociopath claims, so they believe the lies. When the true victim finds out what has been said, everyone has already turned against her.

A victim's forum once offered suggestions on how to handle a smear campaign. For example:

> If anyone tries to talk to you about him, hold up your hand (like a stop sign) and say something like, "I don't want to hear anything about him. He's lying." Say no more. If it continues, say, "My lawyer recommends I warn people they will have to testify where they heard that, should this turn into a libel or slander lawsuit." Watch them scatter quickly when hearing this. This can cause people to stop cold and have another look at what they've been told.

Some more ideas: Say nothing but burst out with raucous laughter, slap your knee and laugh like crazy. "You should have heard what he said about his ex-girlfriend (ex-wife, you, his sister)." You get the idea.

Your own pre-emptive action

Once your relationship falls apart and you realize you're deal-ing with a sociopath, or once you start to hear the lies, you may want to take your own pre-emptive action. Warn your family, friends, co-workers and the Human Resources Department at your job that the sociopath may start saying terrible things about you. This may work if their perceptions haven't already been poi-soned by the sociopath.

It may help to be able to explain why a person would say such terrible things. The reason, of course, is that the person is a so-ciopath. But as we all know, very few people understand what that means. To help others comprehend what you are dealing with, send them a link to Lovefraud.

If you must fight a sociopath, you cannot be nice

Sociopaths do not believe that the rules apply to them. They do not fight fair.

Therefore, if you choose to fight a sociopath, or if you have no choice but to fight a sociopath, your own fighting style will need to become aggressive as well.

If you're a nice person, if you typically want to do what's fair for everyone involved — well, that doesn't work with a sociopath. A sociopath's objective is not to be fair. It's to win, and possibly annihilate you in the process.

To survive the battle, you'll need to act in a way that is probably contrary to your nature. It will be uncomfortable, but necessary.

First decision — do you fight?

Here's the first and most important decision: Do you fight at all?

Typically, fighting means a legal battle. Here are a few things you need to know about going to court against a sociopath:

- Sociopaths love going to court. Often they'll be cool and collected, while you have a meltdown, which makes you look bad.
- Sociopaths often hire sociopathic attorneys, so they'll be tag-teaming you.
- Sociopaths lie in court. They also get witnesses to lie,

either knowingly or unknowingly.
- Judges frequently don't understand sociopaths and may not see through the lies.
- Court costs money. Sociopaths will keep the battle going until you no longer have the money to fight.
- You may know the truth, but may not be able to prove it. Justice may not prevail.

Staying engaged

As I've written many, many times on Lovefraud, the key to recovery from your experience with a sociopath is No Contact. You have to get the person out of your life, and then out of your head.

If you are fighting a battle with a sociopath, you are still engaged. This person and this effort will continue to drain your energy. It is difficult to move on with your recovery.

So here's the critical decision: What course of action will lead to your recovery the fastest? Even though you want justice, would it be better for you to write off your losses, walk away and start over?

Also, is your physical safety at risk? If the sociopath is violent, do you need to flee to protect your life?

Forced to fight

Some people insist that you should never fight a sociopath; they are so evil that it is impossible to win. I don't necessarily agree with that. I've heard from plenty of people who have won.

Yes, perhaps you should just leave. But sometimes standing up for yourself is the best way to achieve recovery. Sometimes you have to fight in order to protect yourself or the people you love. And sometimes sociopaths leave you no choice — they start the fight, and you have to defend yourself.

So if you are going to battle a sociopath, there will be times when you need to fight fire with fire.

Acting differently

Sociopaths tend to target people who are cooperative, considerate, and forthright citizens. These are wonderful traits — but not necessarily helpful when it comes to battling someone who has none of them.

You're going to need to think and act differently.

At the very least, you need to be guarded. Do not tell the sociopath what you are going to do. Do not tell anyone who might talk to the sociopath what you are going to do.

Do not worry about the sociopath's welfare. Do not try to protect him or her. I assure you, the sociopath is not worrying about you.

Do not assume that the sociopath wants to do the right thing, even when children are invovled. For the sociopath, winning is everything, no matter who gets hurt.

Following the rules

Sociopaths, as I said earlier, do not believe that the rules apply to them. Therefore, if you believe in following the rules, you are at a disadvantage in dealing with a sociopath.

For example, suppose you want a divorce. If you were married to a normal person, you could talk to your spouse, agree that the marriage was over, agree to split your bank accounts right down the middle, and you would both get half of the money.

If you were married to a sociopath, your best bet would be to decide on your own that you want the divorce, go to the bank and get your half of the money (or more), retain a lawyer and then serve the sociopath with divorce papers. You should not inform the sociopath in advance that you want a divorce, because once you got to the bank, all of the money would be gone.

In fighting a sociopath, sometimes you may need to bend the rules. Sometimes you may need to act first and worry about the rules later. I don't necessarily want to recommend that you break the law, but you do need to realize that laws may not serve you. If you're worried about violence or some other crime, remember that something bad has to happen before the police can take action.

I definitely had to bend the rules in dealing with my sociopathic ex-husband. If you want to learn what I did, I tell my whole story in my book, *Love Fraud*.

Aggressive action

Sociopaths only understand power. Perhaps you've been beaten down so long that you don't feel like you have any. Surprisingly, this may actually be a source of power, because the sociopath will underestimate you.

Make up your mind. Don't reveal your plans. Figure out where you can push the envelope. Then when you're ready, hit the sociopath with everything you've got. The element of surprise can help you win the fight.

If you must battle a sociopath, there is no win-win. You cannot be nice. You may need to find the strength for bold, aggressive action.

Dear Friend: Please do not take back your sociopathic partner

Editor's note: This is the letter that everyone who has broken up with a sociopathic partner should receive. (It refers to the sociopath as "he," but the sociopath can also be "she.")

Dear Friend,

We've known each other for a long time. We've been there for each other through thick and thin. I care about you, even though I haven't been able to spend much time with you recently — ever since he came into your life.

I heard that the two of you have broken up. I'm thrilled.

Are you surprised? Did you expect me to be upset about your breakup? I'm not. The guy is no good for you. In fact, he's no good for anyone.

You may not want to hear this, but the person who you thought was the love of your life is a sociopath.

But, you say, he can't be a sociopath — sociopaths are serial killers, and he's never killed anyone.

I'm afraid you're mistaken. Yes, some sociopaths are killers, but most of them are not. In reality, a sociopath is a social predator. These people live their lives by exploiting others.

This man has been exploiting you.

He moved in with you — quickly. You told me that he was going to split expenses — how is that working out? I'm willing to bet he hasn't paid you a dime.

If he did pay you, I'm sure he exploited you in other ways.

Were you a babysitter for his kids? Did you do all the cooking and cleaning? Did he want to meet your business connections? Did he ask you for money?

Or was it just the sex? Did he start out all hot and heavy, and then seem to lose interest? In fact, has he been disappearing? Coming up with excuses to be out of town? Or maybe he doesn't ever bother with excuses — he just disappears.

The reason, my friend, is probably that he's been cheating on you. Sociopaths almost always cheat.

Perhaps you knew this in your heart for a long time, but you didn't want to believe it. Finally, the evidence was indisputable and you threw him out. Or maybe he dumped you. Either way, please look at it the way I do: Good riddance.

I know this is hard on you, because you really cared about him. You thought you finally met the person you've been waiting for all your life. I'm sure that's what he told you. How do I know? Because sociopaths say that to everyone. Did he say you were "soul mates"? That's another standard line.

But you thought he was authentic. Why? Because you're authentic. You would never say anything like that unless you meant it. So it's really hard for you to comprehend that someone could say words like, "I love you," and not mean them.

Sociopaths are not capable of love. But they know that if they say, "I love you," they get what they want. Like I said, exploitation.

And now he's calling you again. Saying that he really does love you. He realizes that he made a mistake, and lost the best thing that ever happened to him. He says he's sorry. He says he'll go to therapy. He promises to change.

Blah, blah, blah.

You're confused. He seems to mean it. After all, he's never apologized before. (Hello? Why is that?) And even though the two of you have been fighting for a long time, he never agreed to go to therapy before.

Don't bother. Here's what you need to know: Once sociopaths are adults, there is no rehabilitation. His offer to go to therapy is just a ploy to reel you in again. Why would he do that? My guess is that his new target threw him out, and he needs a place to stay.

But, you say, you really love him. My friend, what you are feeling isn't love, it's addiction. Relationships with sociopaths are highly addictive. The psychological bond that forms with them is really difficult to break. The only way to do it is cold turkey.

So I want you to be strong. Do not take him back. Understand this: He will never change. He might be the charming person that you first met for awhile, but sooner or later, his obnoxious behavior will return. In fact, it will be worse than ever.

And you'll be more depleted than ever, so when he starts demeaning you again, it will be much harder to escape.

My advice is No Contact. Do not talk to this man. Block his texts and emails. Do not visit his Facebook page. If he shows up at your house, call the police.

The longer you stay away from him, the more the fog will lift and your head will clear.

You see, all those nice things he said to you in the beginning, all the promises that he made, were lies. His objective was to reel you in so that he could exploit you. He was successful before, and if you let him back in, he'll do it again.

How, you may ask, can I say this? How do I know what he'll do?

I know because I was in a relationship just like the one that you were in. I learned the hard way, and I don't want you to go through what I went through.

I'm writing you the letter that I wish someone had written to me.

Love always,
Your friend

Identifying sociopathic behavior is easy; giving advice is hard

Just about every day, Lovefraud receives email from readers who are looking for answers about confusing, contradictory and abusive behavior exhibited by people in their lives. The new readers don't understand what they are dealing with; they just tell, either in a few paragraphs or lengthy compositions, their stories. The emails describe some, or many, of the following behaviors:

- Pathological lying
- Pity plays
- Shallow emotions
- Devalue and discard
- Cheating or promiscuity
- Addiction to drugs or alcohol
- Controlling demands
- Financial irresponsibility
- Manipulation of children
- Broken promises
- Claims of "you made me do it"
- Pleas of "I'll never do it again"

The readers ask, "Am I involved with a sociopath?"

For those of us who now know what sociopathic behavior looks like, it is apparent that the answer is yes—or that at least the readers are describing sociopathic traits.

More than 10,000 people have contacted Lovefraud with their

stories—and others have told their stories in comments posted on this blog. In all of them, the same behavior patterns are described over and over again. In fact, many of you have wondered (facetiously) if you were all involved with the same person.

Asking for advice

When newbies, who have been confused by lies and broken promises, learn that there is a personality disorder that describes what they've been dealing with, they have a few reactions. One is relief that they are not crazy — they really are experiencing irrational demands and covert manipulation.

Another is horror at the magnitude of the problems they face — especially upon learning that there really isn't any treatment for a sociopath. With that, the new reader starts asking for advice, and this is where things get tricky.

Here are questions that I've been asked:

- He's threatened to kill me—will he do it?
- How do I get the judge to see the truth?
- How can I get the authorities to arrest her?
- How can I protect my children?
- How can I get my money back?
- What should I do?

As much as I wish that any of us who are further along the road of understanding could answer these questions, the reality is, we can't.

Each situation is unique

Although we often see the same patterns of behavior, each sociopath is unique. Each victim is unique. Each situation is unique. As victims try to extricate themselves from entanglements with sociopaths, any and all of these issues may be pivotal:

- How much clout does the sociopath have in the community?
- How well can the sociopath manipulate the legal sys-

tem?
- How much money does the sociopath have to throw into the conflict?
- Who believes the sociopath?
- Who can the sociopath make into allies?
- Are there any witnesses? Will they speak up?
- How old are the children?
- What office politics are involved?
- Do legal authorities take the case seriously?
- Are there any ties that can't be broken?
- How much money does the victim have (remaining)?
- How much strength does the victim have to continue the battle?

Sometimes I feel so helpless. I can offer some generalizations about what sociopaths tend to do — based on the 10,000 cases I've learned about — but I cannot predict what any particular sociopath will do, how authorities may react, or if anyone will see through the deceptions. All of this makes it very difficult to give advice.

Solitary journey

In reality, extricating ourselves, recovering from, and coming to terms with the sociopath(s) in our life is a solitary journey. Other people may make suggestions, but we must ultimately make the decisions on how to cope.

And sometimes the range of the choices we have the ability to make is very narrow. A judge may decide on joint custody of children, or even award custody to the sociopath. Law enforcement may decline to investigate or prosecute. If we win our case in civil court, we may never collect a judgment.

In situations like these, decisions are taken away from us.

When that happens, our only choices have to do with our own attitude. Are we going to let the sociopath sink us? Or are we going to somehow find a way to heal?

Real response is internal

There is great wisdom in the adage, "This, too, shall pass."

It's been almost 20 years since I left my sociopathic ex-husband. I've processed most of the emotional trauma associated with the experience, so it doesn't have the grip on me that it once did. In fact, if it weren't for the fact that I'm running Lovefraud, it would have no grip on me at all.

Twenty years ago, I was on the phone with another woman scammed by my husband multiple times a day. Although we are still friends, now we rarely speak. She's moved on in her life—the experience is a distant memory.

The same thing happens here at Lovefraud. In the midst of their trauma, readers post frequently. But eventually we stop seeing their names and comments. I hope that means they've left the experience behind.

In the end, the real response to the experience with the sociopath is internal. We have to come to terms with the betrayal, the injury, the exploitation. So although it's hard to give foolproof advice for dealing with the circumstances that the predator creates in our lives, the truly important advice is this: Find a way to heal yourself.

10 reasons to roll your eyes at sociopaths

Everything sociopaths say is for effect. They are not capable of honest communication — every statement has an agenda.

If you have sociopaths in your life, your objective is to get to the point that you simply do not take them seriously. When they are making promises, don't hope that this time they'll really come through. Your reaction should be, "Yeah, right."

When you hear any of these statements, the best thing you can do is roll your eyes:

1. I love you

Impossible — sociopaths are not capable of love

2. I'll never do it again

Yes, they will — although it may take a while. Sociopaths can control their behavior, so if they need to walk the straight and narrow temporarily to convince you to stay, they will. But eventually they will do whatever they did again.

3. Trust me

No, no, NO! These people absolutely cannot be trusted with anything!

4. You're crazy, mentally ill, and should be on meds

This is a typical sociopathic strategy. They will tell you that you're mentally unbalanced. They will often say this with such concern in their voices that you think they're really worried about you. NO! They're trying to destroy you.

5. Other people think you're crazy, mentally ill, and should be on meds

Another typical strategy. They'll tell you all the terrible things that other people are supposedly saying about you. You, of course, become upset and embarrassed, and never ask these people what they really think. But the other people never made the statements! Sociopaths do this to erode your support system and isolate you.

6. I'll go for therapy

No, they probably won't go. And it doesn't matter anyway, because once a sociopath is an adult, there is no rehabilitation.

7. I'll never cheat again

Yes, they will. Cheating and promiscuity are ingrained in this disorder. In fact, they may be cheating even as they make the statement. They don't stop.

8. You're cheating with your co-worker, neighbor, the repairman

Sociopaths often vehemently accuse you of cheating. Your natural reaction is to defend yourself. Remember they are doing this for effect! They probably know you aren't cheating, but they want to undermine you. (If you are cheating, never, ever confess!)

9. You must forgive because the Bible says so

Sociopaths often pretend to be born again, religious, spiritual or pious. They are not. They don't care about religion. But they will use religious teachings in order to assert control over you.

10. I'll kill myself

If you hear this statement, either the sociopath is lying, and just wants to make you feel guilty. Or the sociopath is serious. Either way, you cannot solve the problem. The best thing you can do is call 911.

Recognize that nothing sociopaths say is sincere, and the best thing you can do is ignore anything that comes out of their mouths with one exception. If sociopaths threaten you, pay attention. If they threaten to hurt you, ruin your job, take your kids and you sense they are capable of these actions — take precautions.

But when sociopaths are saying whatever they can think of to hook you again, well, just roll your eyes.

Dealing with sociopaths: Fight or flight?

Sociopaths are social predators who live their lives by exploiting people. When you're the person who has been exploited, how should you respond? Do you try to hold the sociopath accountable? Or do you cut your losses and run?

Lovefraud is an open forum, with many people expressing opinions about what you should do. In the past, some folks have posted comments saying give up, run away, don't fight, you can't win.

I don't necessarily agree with that. Yes, in some cases, fleeing is the best course of action. But sometimes the only way to survive is to fight. Or sometimes standing up to the sociopath enables you to reclaim yourself, even if you don't win the battle.

I believe you should do what is best for you. But figuring out "what is best" may be difficult. You need to carefully evaluate the entire situation before deciding what, if any, action to take. The following considerations may help you.

If you suffered financial losses

Do you have documentation that the sociopath promised to repay you? If you don't have an agreement in writing, it will be very difficult to pursue your claim. The sociopath may argue — convincingly — that the money was a gift.

Does the sociopath have any money, property or assets that you can go after? Does he or she have a job? If the sociopath has nothing, there may be no point.

How much will it cost you to go after what he or she owes you? Is the amount of money taken from you worth the trouble it will be to get it back?

Can you use small claims court? The good news about small claims court is that you don't need to pay for an attorney. If the sociopath owes you more than the dollar limit for small claims cases, perhaps you can break it up into several different claims. Again, you will need documentation.

Even if you won't be able to collect, you may want to file a lawsuit against the sociopath just to expose him or her, or create a public record. This does, in a way, hold the sociopath accountable, even if you are never repaid.

Criminal behavior

Is the sociopath engaged in criminal behavior? Is the sociopath dangerous? Can you report the behavior without jeopardizing your own safety? Are you willing to cooperate with law enforcement agencies? Or, is there a tip line where you can report the behavior anonymously?

Would your conscience bother you if you did not report the behavior?

If the sociopath is accusing you of criminal behavior, you must fight. Do not admit to any criminal behavior that you did not commit. A criminal record can ruin your life.

Children with a sociopath

Having children with a sociopath is a nightmare. The best thing that can happen is for the sociopath to go away. You may want to offer a deal — if your former partner will give up parental rights, you won't ask for child support. Usually this deal won't cost you anything, because sociopaths drag their feet on paying child support.

Many sociopaths, however, will not give up parental rights. They want to use the kids to continue to control you.

The issues involved in co-parenting with a sociopath are incredibly complex, and beyond the scope of this article. So here are just a few suggestions:

Document everything. Keep very good records of everything that happens. Save every text, email, receipt and record. You never know what you will need.

During a custody case, do not let any false claims that the sociopath makes about you go unchallenged in court. If you do not challenge the lies, the statements become part of the court record and will cause problems for you later.

Make your custody agreement as comprehensive as possible. Then, you follow it to the letter and demand that the sociopath follow it.

As Quinn Pierce wrote in an article, avoiding conflict to keep the peace may not work, and can hurt both you and the kids. But remember, the sociopath's objective is to get a reaction out of you. So be calm, unemotional and businesslike as you enforce your boundaries. Even when the sociopath upsets you, never let him or her see it.

Your physical and emotional strength

If you were involved with a sociopath, you certainly were deceived, manipulated and betrayed. You may have been physically assaulted. You may have endured emotional and psychological injury.

So as you're considering fight or flight, what can you really handle right now?

Your first priority must be your own health and safety. If you need to give up the money or property you lost in order to protect your very life, then do it.

Or maybe you need to retreat for the time being. Then, after taking time to recover and gather your strength, you can go after the sociopath later. That is perfectly acceptable.

Recovery and accountability

True recovery from a sociopath means moving forward with your life. It may not be the same life that you had before the sociopath. In fact, if you work on deep emotional healing because of this experience, it could even be a better life.

So what is the best way for you to move forward? Is it letting go of what happened? Or is it standing up for yourself and holding the sociopath accountable? Is it letting go on some issues and taking a stand on others? Only you can decide.

Here's another factor: Sociopaths will continue with their exploitative behavior as long as they keep getting away with it. If nothing else, I hope we can at least talk about our experiences. As more people realize that millions of predators live among us, perhaps working to hold sociopaths accountable won't feel as lonely as it does now.

My experience with fighting

Personally, I am glad that I fought, although I did not claim a total victory. When I divorced my ex-husband, the judge awarded me all the money I claimed — $227,000 — plus $1 million in punitive damages. I spent a year and even more money trying to serve my judgment. I failed, and eventually had to declare bankruptcy.

But I did prove in court that he committed fraud. That legal judgment enabled me to expose James Montgomery for the con artist that he is. And, it enabled me to create Lovefraud, where I use my experience to try to educate the world about the social predators who live among us.

For me, the fight was worth it.

Approaching someone who has been burned by a sociopath

Lovefraud received the following email from a man whom we'll call "Andrew."

I recently met a lady out of the blue after I had sat at home alone for 2 years. She is the victim of a sociopath — reads & posts on the Lovefraud site trying to heal. She says she can't tell me all the damage done & I don't need to know — it's her business unless she feels she needs to share.

She had cabin fever — had to get out for a night — hence our meeting. Well I had basically given up on finding someone until I met her. We instantly clicked. It was so good for 3 weeks —making plans of fun things to do. I thought it would help her heal — to go have fun again.

I think she started liking me too much in that short period of time — got scared & slammed on the brakes. She says she needs time, but truly values my friendship & adores me. I'm trying to give her "time." It's so hard when she lit up my life for a while.

She wants to see me again, but doesn't know when.

I have no motives other than to get to know her & help her get over the past. She might just be the one if we spend the time to know one another.

I have read the Lovefraud blog trying to understand — some really sad stories.

What should I do?

In the thousands of emails that I've received, this is the first time someone has asked this question (which I've paraphrased) — how do you approach a potential romantic partner when that person has been burned by a sociopath? I appreciate that fact that Andrew cared enough to ask the question.

I will answer the question assuming that everything is exactly as presented — a woman, whom we'll call Caroline, had a terrible experience with a sociopath and is skittish about opening herself to another man. Andrew honestly likes Caroline, and wants to get to know her better. I will assume that neither Andrew nor Caroline is actually a predator who is looking for a new source of supply.

This, of course, is something that Caroline, and everyone else who has been betrayed and damaged by a sociopath, needs to understand and believe: There are good people in the world. Yes, as many as 12 percent of the population are social predators—sociopaths, psychopaths, narcissists, borderlines. But that still means that 88 percent of the world's people are not disordered, and are capable of having a loving relationship.

Understand where she's been

So, Andrew, the first thing for you to understand is that Caroline has been through the meat grinder. She's experienced betrayal that has rocked her to her core. She's certainly suffered emotional and psychological abuse, and may have also suffered verbal, physical, sexual and financial abuse. In fact, it may be a miracle that she is still standing.

If you've never experienced this level of betrayal — most people haven't — it may be hard for you to believe what she's gone through. Should she tell you anything about what happened, it may sound like a bad movie, and you may be inclined to think she is exaggerating. I assure you, when someone is involved with a sociopath, anything is possible. I've collected more than 10,000 cases, and many of the stories should be made into movies. You can't make this stuff up.

Caroline, however, is accustomed to not being believed. She may have gone to court and to the police, and they didn't believe her story. It's possible her friends or her own family do not believe her. So one of the best things you can do is believe her. It will help her feel validated.

Go slow

Andrew, you will need take things very slowly. It's likely that the sociopath swept into Caroline's life in a whirlwind romance — if you call all the time, if you are overly exuberant about wanting to see her, it may set off alarm bells, because that's how the sociopath acted. Let her set the pace. Keep things light.

Understand that trust needs to be earned. This may be why Caroline got into trouble in the first place — she trusted too readily. Now, she may have gone too far in the other direction, and resolved to never trust anyone again. This is an unhealthy position, because we do need to be able to trust in order to live a good life. But you may not know how much progress Caroline has made in regaining her ability to trust.

So if you want to move forward, you need to be trustworthy. Tell her the truth about everything. Keep your promises. Call when you say you're going to call, and show up when you promise that you'll show up. In fact, I hope that's how you live your life anyway.

It may not work

Finally, it is possible that Caroline simply is not recovered enough to think about another involvement. If she tells you that she really can't be in a relationship, don't argue with her, and don't take it personally. You may just need to accept it and move on.

But if Caroline indicates that does want to get to know you, albeit slowly, getting closer will probably be worth the wait. Before hooking up with the sociopath, Caroline was probably loving, giving, caring, responsible, dynamic and empathetic — because that's the type of person that sociopaths target. So if she's able to find herself, and open herself — well, it could be rewarding for both of you.

Doing battle with sociopaths

Today, July 4th, is Independence Day in the United States of America. On this day 235 years ago, the country's forefathers declared independence from the tyranny of a distant king. Today, let us all declare independence from the tyranny of sociopaths.

Declaring independence, of course, is only the beginning of the struggle. In 1776, the tyrant did not want to lose a prized possession — the Colonies — and retaliated by sending an army. The Colonists who believed in independence had no choice but to fight, even though most had little experience — they were farmers, tradesmen and laborers. But they learned how to fight. It took five years, many battles and many hardships, but in the end, the United States of America emerged victorious.

What can we learn from those Colonists that we can use in our own battles? The early Americans believed in themselves, believed in their cause, and did not give up. Oh, they suffered defeats, but they retreated, regrouped, and fought again. They learned from their mistakes, found allies and kept going.

If you're doing battle with a sociopath — and make no mistake, any interaction is a battle — here are some strategies that will help you:

1. Know your enemy. Be brutally honest in evaluating the sociopath in your life. Remember: The sociopath never loved you. All you ever were to him or her was a source of supply. Once you get over the shock of their soullessness, you'll begin to see the patterns of their actions. This will enable you to predict what they will do, and plan accordingly.

2. Never underestimate the sociopath. Do not anticipate that the sociopath will act as you, a person capable of love and empathy, would act. The sociopath has no concern for your emotions, your feelings and your welfare. Without empathy or a conscience, the sociopath is capable of doing anything, even the unthinkable, to get what he or she wants, which is to win.

3. Conserve your own resources. You can't fight if you are sick or injured, so do your best to take care of yourself. Eat right; avoid drugs and alcohol; get enough rest. If you are suffering from anxiety or depression, a good way to relieve them is through exercise. Be gentle with yourself as you recover from trauma.

4. Plan strategically. Figure out what you really want and need, and figure out a way to get them. Never let the sociopath know your plans. If you are living with the person and need to escape, prepare a getaway bag and leave when he or she is not around. If you are going to court, keep careful records and document everything that happens. Keep in mind that you may need to use subterfuge and diversion to execute your plans.

5. Pick your battles. Determine what is really important to you, and what you can let go of. Your life and health are important; you may need to give up on recovering your money, saving your reputation or seeing justice done—at least for the time being. Only take on the battles that are vitally important at the moment.

6. Use overwhelming force. If you do have an opportunity to serve justice, go after the sociopath with everything you've got. Do not play nice; do not hold back. The harder you hit, the more likely your chances of success.

7. Seek peace. Remember, the only life you absolutely, positively can influence is your own. Your ultimate objective should be your peace of mind and peace of heart. Achieving it may mean letting go of material goods, people and past traumas. You may need to redefine yourself and how you relate to the world. If you can get to a place of tranquility, you are victorious.

Letter to Lovefraud: Countermeasures to deal with the sociopathic ex

Editor's note: Here is a letter from a Lovefraud reader whom we'll call "GI Joe." This reader is in the military, so July 4th seemed an appropriate time to post this article. First, I want to acknowledge him and all members of the military for their service. Secondly, the answers to his questions have to do with freedom.

My ex-wife and I divorced in 2012. The marriage was a nightmare that lasted more than 11 years and left me financially ruined, emotionally distressed and alone. To make matters worse, my ex moved out of state with my children, making it impossible for me to see my children on a regular basis.

Since I was in a financial hurt locker, it took me years before I was able to save up enough to battle her in court to get full summer vacations with the children, every other Christmas holiday, and guaranteed phone calls and skype calls. She even has to pay half on travel costs for the children to come see me.

In spite of all of this, my sociopathic ex finds ways to make my life difficult and further alienate me from the children. Pictures of my children and I that were hanging on their bedroom walls were removed. My ex spath even went so far as to instruct our children to begin calling her new boyfriend (now her husband) "daddy," causing more confusion for the children (especially my 5-year-old daughter, who now differentiates her stepfather and myself as "fake daddy and real daddy").

To even make matters worse, I receive no financial support from my ex while the children are with me, to include the fact that my ex is also keeping the child support I send to her. So with this being said, I have to support myself and three children (ages 12, 11 and 5) all while serving in the military, which bears a pretty large financial burden in the form of day care expenses.

To top this off, even though I pay my ex over $16,000 a year in child support, I don't even get to claim them on taxes as our divorce decree did not specify this and my ex files for taxes before I can even say anything about it. Last year, my ex filed her taxes with her husband and claimed all three of my children, to include one child she has with her new husband. She does not work, and her husband is also in the military. By doing this, she ensures that I am not able to accrue large amounts of money, keeping me from financially stabilizing myself and also ensuring that I will not be able to afford going to court in order to rectify these wrongs.

My question is, How do I allow myself to heal when I am still very much in contact with my ex spath? How can you heal when you cannot defend yourself?

If I do as yourself and other writers have suggested and partake in a no-contact order, then I risk losing my children and/or allowing them to become brainwashed by my ex. I know I have to go to court again with her because as long as things stay the way they are, I will never be able to get on my feet and it will become increasingly harder for me to spend time with my children as I will not be able to do so financially.

How do you maintain that arm's distance to allow the healing process to begin? I believe very much so that this issue needs to be resolved in order for me to truly move on.

Donna Andersen responds

GI Joe:

Know that what you are experiencing is typical when you're trying to co-parent with a sociopath. Often the sociopath's objective is to do everything she can to make your life miserable. So let's talk about, to borrow a military term, countermeasures.

Your letter brings up three issues:

- Dealing with your ex-wife
- Dealing with your children
- Your own recovery

I'll discuss these issues one at a time.

The ex-wife

Yes, usually Lovefraud recommends no contact with the sociopath. The big exception to that policy is when you share children with him or her. Then your objective needs to be minimizing the contact, and making whatever contact you do have less stressful.

The only communication you should have with her should be related to the "business" of dealing with your children. If she tries to engage you in any other discussion, do not take the bait. Do not reveal anything about your life.

Even though it is sad that she is out of state and it's difficult to see your kids, the good news is that she is not in your face. This should make it easier to attain what I call "emotional no contact."

Emotional no contact means you do not let her get to you. When she pulls her latest stunt, whatever it is, you simply do not react. Remember, sociopaths feed on reactions. So if you deny her a reaction, you are not feeding the beast.

You want to get to the point where you can anticipate what she's going to do, and when she does it, you privately roll your eyes. In your mind you should be saying, "There she goes again."

Maybe you're already doing this, and if so, that's great. If you're not, getting to this point has to do with your own healing, which I'll discuss in a bit.

About the money — first of all, perhaps it's better to use your money to see your children under the arrangements that exist now, rather then spending it on lawyers. You could spend thousands of dollars to go to court, and end up with a situation that changes very little.

If what you really want is to be able to claim your kids as a tax deduction, maybe there's another way to accomplish that. Can you call the IRS, explain your situation, and ask for a "clarification"? It won't cost anything. And who knows? Maybe the IRS will become curious about what else she's doing with her taxes.

Finally, document, document, document. Keep very good records of anything that happens to your children, and any inappropriate parenting by your ex. Save every email, text and document. Keep notes, and develop a way to organize them. Should you ever decide that she is abusing your kids, and you must to go back to court, you'll need evidence to prove your case.

The children

You want to be a beacon of love and stability for your children. Every time you speak to them, tell them that you love them. Make sure you are reliable and keep your promises. (Their sociopathic mother won't do either.) Call when you say you're going to call. Do what you say you're going to do.

Your kids will see the difference. After all, your youngest already knows the difference between "real daddy" and "fake daddy."

About the pictures — can you make a Facebook or Pinterest page where you can post them? This can be a reminder for your kids that is always available. Keep updating the page with messages and pictures. (For safety's sake, make sure the page is private.)

Because the American family courts are often a fiasco, many, many parents have seen their kids court-ordered to live with sociopaths. It can be hard on the kids. But eventually they grow up, and I've heard kids who have "aged out" of the situation talk about their experience. Here's what they say to the healthy parent: Don't give up. Keep being there for your kids, however you can.

If the kids aren't themselves disordered — which, unfortunately, is a risk — eventually they will see the truth.

Your recovery

In your letter, you said that you feel the financial issue needs to be resolved in order for you to truly move on. Actually, this is not true.

Recovery from the experience with a sociopath takes two tracks. The first track is dealing with whatever practical mess the sociopath left for you. The second track is your personal healing.

Here's what you should understand: You do not need to wait until your financial situation is resolved to begin your emotional recovery. You can make progress on both of these tracks at the same time.

I wrote about this a few months ago in the following Lovefraud article, *Recovery — parallel courses for moving forward.*

Acceptance

Most of our upset after tangling with a sociopath comes from wanting things to be different. We wish that we never met the person. We wish we'd gotten out when we sensed something was wrong. We wish that the sociopath could just be normal.

The key to recovery is acceptance. This does not mean that you condone the sociopath's behavior. But you do accept that the situation is what it is.

Then you grieve it.

Processing the pain

You've experienced a terrible loss — the same as losing friends in Afghanistan or Iraq. You've lost the woman you thought you married, the family life that you wanted, the joy of being with your children every day, the future that you envisioned. Make no mistake — the loss is severe.

You'll need to process the grief, which means allowing yourself to feel the pain. If you've done this, great. If not, realize that when emotions are bottled up inside of you, they fester. They affect the way you perceive life. And if the pain is stuck within you long enough, your body turns it into disease.

Give yourself permission to process the pain, knowing that getting the negative emotions out of your system frees you.

When you feel better, you may start to see new solutions to the practical matters you're faced with. You'll also be able to offer more love to your children — and that's really important.

Is this man insecure, a jerk or a sociopath?

Editor's Note: This letter to Lovefraud is submitted by the Lovefraud reader who goes by the name "Shanmoo." Donna Andersen's comments follow the letter.

I can't believe I've had to come back here after five years. I had a spath boyfriend in 2008-2009, and spent many a night on this site. However, I did move forward, and I believed I had dealt with all the issues, karma and justice happened and in fact I met a decent guy. Unfortunately we went our separate ways because of my illness, at that time.

My relationship with co-worker "A"
And that brings me to this guy, we'll call him "A". We are broken up now, and he is basically being an absolute jerk, I work with him, and I need your help to deal with him. I'm having to find another job and it's just not right.

Two and one half years ago I had to move back to my home country after a life abroad, due to illness. I have fibromyalgia. I took a job here in the UK, well below my qualifications. It was better than fighting the disability benefits system. About 16 months ago I met my now ex — "A" — in my workplace. I used to walk past him, and I remember him just staring at me; watching me as I went past, almost obsessively. He is quite attractive.

Anyway, I used to see him in the work kitchen and one

day I figured, just talk to him. So I did. Well that was that. He used to watch me from his desk. He could see to the kitchen, and every time I went in there, he would turn up, and talk to me. This went on for weeks. I wondered, when is he going to ask me out? Then I got collared by his friend's wife, who also works in there, and she said he had been talking about me and if he asked me out, would I say yes, well of course. She told me that in all the years they had known him, he had never gone out with, or been bothered about any woman. She assured me he would treat me well. Anyway I engineered things a bit. I asked him along to a mutual night out with friends. That night he asked me to go out the next night and I said yes and that was that.

We started seeing each other, and honestly, it was really good, although he wasn't your average man. He was a bit useless. A very longterm bachelor, and didn't really have any home skills. I was decorating my flat at the time and I was shocked that he had never held a paintbrush in his life. I had to teach a 41-year-old man how to paint. He also didn't drive, which I found a bit odd.

He used to message me and be with me loads though. I can't complain. However after about five or six weeks he landed a bombshell. He sat me down and told me the relationship wasn't working for him. I didn't understand this as we had been getting on great especially in the bedroom but he told me he felt that we were just friends. It brought me to tears. I was really upset. He apologized and said he didn't want to upset me and asked me to forget it. He said he had just misunderstood stuff. Women had previously treated him like second best.... etc.

Anyway we just plodded on and really things were good.

An invitation to move in

Four months into the relationship and he was asking me to move in with him in a new place, and have his baby.... which I thought was a bit soon to be honest. However I am 45 years old.

The one main thing however that bugged me was the driving license. Now admittedly I wasn't in a great place as in March this year my fibromyalgia flared up and it was really bad, I was in so much pain and I started to feel resentful. He had promised me that he would learn to drive, and in April, he told me that he had never wanted to learn to drive and just said to avoid an argument.

So I took him out at the car park in work, and told him to basically f*** off and be single, for lying to me. I didn't really want to break up with him; it was a cry for help. I couldn't manage everything. However, he just walked away. I tried to work things out with him two days later and he told me that he had wanted to break up with me months ago? He said I had been so negative for months and he is a laid back positive person.

I found that a bit of a joke; as most nights when he had been at my house I had been listening to him complain about various people at work incessantly, also just before going to sleep!

The breakup

To cut a long story short, the last five months have been absolute hell. He has treated me like complete rubbish since our breakup.

Initially after the breakup I tried to get things working again. I went to see him, accepted my part, that I had been wrong to push him to learn to drive, and we talked loads. It was good. At one point his barriers came down and he held my hand. But then he said, "oh we will just be friends." I thought this a bit odd?

Friends didn't work. He basically treated me hot and cold, as he wanted. Would be nice to me, then just ignore me and blank me. So I went to his flat about three months ago and had it out with him big style. It came out in the row that he was very angry about the way we had broken up. Ok, fair enough. However I told him never to speak to me again. So what did he do? Two days later in work when he saw me, sparked up a conversation with me, as if it had never happened.

A difficult work environment

We didn't speak for three weeks, and it was just awful. Being in the same workplace and having mutual friends. I could see from going by him in the office that he was bothered. The atmosphere was terrible, especially around mutual friends and when I needed to go by him. Someone suggested that we go out for a coffee and put the past behind us. When I suggested it, he seemed up for it, and then went weird, so we ended up falling out about that!

However eventually we met up and you know what, we had a great afternoon. We spent three hours together and it was great. He left with a big smile; walked with me towards my car. Next day in work he was beaming. We had loads of contact. He was protective. He was interested in me. He cared what was going on. After that there has been some chat, often consisting of him following me to the kitchen, then hooking me into conversations, wanting to know what was going on, and asking question after question.

We went out again three weeks ago... same again, for most of the night. After our coffee he asked me to stay out longer which I did. He walked me to the car park, which was quite a way, but then went weird on me like "bye"... huh? I hadn't asked for anything. He didn't even see me to the car and make sure that I was safe. His excuse was that the lighting seemed good.

Since then he has just got more and more distant, and now he has completely cut me off again. He blanked and ignored me the other day in work!!!

Doing my head in

It is so doing my head in. I have been wanting to leave my job ever since we broke up and now I'm getting desperate.

I raised it with my supervisor today. It is emotional control and abuse. I don't know what I'm going to deal with in work — will he be nice to me, and talk with me, or will he ignore me and blank me, stick his nose up like he can do better? He ignores me in front of other people that we work with? It's horrible.

It's upsetting me and I can no longer work in this environment. You can't work "around" an abusive relationship; the only solution is to get away. However to do that, I need another job. In the meantime, I have to deal with this ****head in the office, five days a week. It's killing me. I am going home most nights in tears. I'm either drinking or on sedatives.

This guy is actually very insecure, but hides it well. Right now his ego is boosted by having had an attractive girlfriend who chased after him.

My life is in tatters, as I'm having to leave a secure job because of his behavior, and my mental health is a mess. He walks around like he is the bee's knees. I try to knock him off his pedestal but nothing works. I'd so like to punch him!

I should tell you that he loves his money. He is obsessed with work and saving, but spends it on nothing. He is a total commitment phobic.

Can you help?

Donna Andersen's comments

Shanmoo, I welcome you back to Lovefraud, although I am sorry for the circumstances that have precipitated your return.

You've asked for help in dealing with "A." Here are my thoughts.

The basic issue is that "A" has been indecisive, ambivalent and sometimes cruel in his involvement with you. Some of his behavior, such as the following, is typical of sociopaths:

- Blaming you for being negative, claiming to be positive, then complaining incessantly
- Breaking up and treating you like rubbish
- Being hot and cold with you
- After a big fight, talking with you as if nothing had happened, then cutting you off again

So is this guy a jerk, insecure, or disordered? Although his actions certainly feel abusive, based on the information you've included in your letter, a clinician might say "A" doesn't quite meet the criteria for a personality disorder. (For more on how to determine if someone is "a sociopath," read, *Sociopaths range from sleazy to serial killer.*)

Guess what? For you, it doesn't matter.

More healing

In my opinion, the fact that "A" came into your life means only one thing: You have more healing to do.

This does not mean that you have failed. In fact, it may indicate that you've made very good progress.

Here's how you started your letter:

> I can't believe I've had to come back here after five years. I had a spath boyfriend in 2008-2009, and spent many a night on this site. However, I did move forward, and I believed I had dealt with all the issues, karma and justice happened and in fact I met a decent guy. Unfortunately we went our separate ways because of my illness, at that time.

I'm sure you did a lot of personal recovery work. If you saw some measure of karma and justice for your sociopathic ex, that's terrific. And if "A," as miserable as he was, wasn't as bad as your previous sociopathic boyfriend, it means your emotional state has actually improved.

But you're not finished.

Deep emotional wounds

Throughout our lifetimes, we can suffer many, many emotional wounds. Some are far worse than others.

Often, we are not in a position to deal with them when they occur. During childhood, for example, we may have had to endure abusive or neglectful parents. Or perhaps our mother and father were simply too exhausted trying to make ends meet to give us the attention we craved. Either of these situations — plus anything else that may have happened — can create deep wounds.

But as children, we often can't do anything about it. We lock the pain up in a corner of our psyche, and do our best to survive.

Then we may have had previous romantic relationships — especially with abusers — that created terrible feelings of disappointment, betrayal and fear. But at the time we may have felt trapped, so again, we stuffed the pain into a psychological closet.

Even romances that end amicably create wounds. You mentioned meeting a "decent guy," but that didn't work out. It's still a disappointment, and you may still be carrying the residue.

Your involvement with "A" was legitimately painful. But I think it has a hidden blessing. As you release the negative emotions of this experience, the pain of other, deeper wounds may also rise to the surface, so you can release them as well.

Be patient

So what do you do now? Cut yourself some slack. Recognize that you are in the thick of this experience, and it will take you some time to recover.

If you're arriving home in tears, that's okay, because that's how you release the pain.

I would advise that you lay off the alcohol. Alcohol is a depressant, so it will make you feel worse. I'd also advise being careful, and consulting your doctor, on the sedatives.

About your job — don't do anything yet. Give yourself some time to process everything. You may soon feel better, and discover that "A" is easily ignored at work.

You may also come to the conclusion that you're better off without him — after all, who wants a man who can't drive and can't paint?

A mother asks: 'What is my responsibility toward my sociopathic adult son?'

Lovefraud received the following letter from a reader whom we'll call, "Margaret Louise."

Please point me in the direction for good advice about recovering from heartache caused by my adult son, who is a sociopath. And, help me realize my responsibilities as his parent.

Joshua is 33 years old. He has 3 children by 3 different women. While he is in the relationship with the women, I am blacklisted from contact with my grandchildren. As the relationships fall apart, and the mothers realize they've been duped, I can begin to have that cherished relationship with my grandchildren and fortunately with the mothers.

Because I have developed a wonderful relationship with Joshua's most recent ex-wife and their 3-year old son, I was seeing more of Joshua and we were able to tolerate each other, even be cordial. However, as he has entered into another new relationship, he has reverted to being cruel and verbally abusive.

It is my opinion that he is trying to wipe his slate and present himself to her as a victim.

I have decided that this is the very last time that I will put myself in this situation with Joshua. My heart aches for giving up on him but I don't think I can take any more rejection and cruelty from him. Also, there is great concern about my role in protecting others that may have to deal with him.

Every time there is a school shooting, mass murder, or other events caused by emotionally sick or mentally ill persons, the public seems to always ask, "Why didn't those in his life do something?"

If this is my responsibility, how do I best go about it? If it is not my responsibility, how do I let go of the guilt?

Of course, I know there are always repercussions from Joshua if I get involved. But, the lives of the others are important. Especially, the children.

And, how likely is Joshua's behavior to become physically dangerous to any of us in his life?

Donna Andersen responds

Margaret Louise,

I am so sorry for what you are going through. I've heard from other parents in your situation, and it is extremely painful.

First I want to address your question about violence. Although the public perceives sociopaths as deranged serial killers, most of them never kill anyone. In fact, plenty of sociopaths are not violent at all — they wreak their havoc psychologically and emotionally.

The best predictor of future behavior is past behavior. Has Joshua been violent in the past? I am referring to any kind of violence — towards people, animals or property. If the answer is yes, there may be reason for concern. If he does not have any history of violence, he is less likely to be violent in the future, although, of course, anything is possible — especially if he gets involved with drugs.

You asked about your responsibilities. Here's how I see it:

1. When you have the opportunity, tell the truth about his behavior

Many parents cover for their disordered adult children. This is one reason why sociopaths who still see their families continue to get away with manipulation and exploitation. Parents and other relatives stay quiet about their disordered children's bad behavior.

This sometimes happens when the sociopath brings home a new love interest. Parents hope the new partner will be the person who finally gets their offspring turned around. Or, parents want the new partner to take the disordered individual off their hands. One Lovefraud reader told me that on the day of her wedding to a man who turned out to be a sociopath, the mother of the groom said to her, "He's your problem now."

It sounds like your eyes are open about your son's behavior. Perhaps you did try to warn some of the women he snagged, and they didn't believe you. This is common — sociopaths are great at impression management and seduction, so it is often difficult for victims to hear warnings from others. All you can do is try.

2. Do not enable him

Some parents of sociopaths keep cleaning up the messes these ruthless manipulators make. I've heard of parents who continuously give their disordered kids money and bail them out of jail.

Sociopaths will exploit anyone, including their parents. They will keep taking as long as you keep giving. If he gets himself in trouble, let him deal with the consequences.

3. Do what you can for your grandchildren

Your son will likely cause upheaval in their lives, and it may be very important for them to know that their grandmother loves them.

However, recognize that your own health and safety come first. If being involved with your grandchildren jeopardizes you, your safety or your peace of mind in any way, you may have to stop contact with them.

Your recovery

As far as your own recovery — please recognize that you have done your best. If you are concerned now about your grandchildren, I am sure that you were concerned about Joshua when he was young, even when he was difficult, as he probably was.

But the time does come when you have to let go. As sad as it is, you have reached that decision.

A mother asks: 'What is my responsibility toward my sociopathic adult son?'

Joshua is an adult now, and he is making his own choices.

This is a bitter loss — perhaps more difficult than death, because he wasn't taken from you; you had to decide to remove him from your life.

You are justifiably heartbroken. So I suggest that you allow yourself to grieve. Allow yourself to feel the disappointment, the betrayal, the pain. It is by feeling the pain that we can move through it, and reach the other side.

Take care of yourself first. If you can safely offer assistance to your grandchildren and their mothers, do that. Then turn your son over to God or whatever higher power is meaningful to you.

When relatives suspect child abuse

A woman contacted Lovefraud seeking advice in dealing with an extremely disturbing situation. This woman, we'll call her Rosalyn, suspects her sister-in-law of child abuse.

Rosalyn has been caring for the child regularly ever since she was small, and the girl is now starting school. The little girl is fine in Rosalyn's care, but when it's time for her go home, when Rosalyn says, "Mommy's coming to get you," the child starts crying and carrying on.

Several times Rosalyn has noticed that the child had bruises. "How did your hurt yourself?" she asked. The girl said she didn't remember. Other incidents also have Rosalyn concerned about her young niece's wellbeing.

Rosalyn sees behavior in her sister-in-law that makes her think the woman is a sociopath. It's not a conclusion she came to lightly. "It took me about a year to figure it out," Rosalyn said. "I'm pretty sure that's what the problem is."

The woman is still married to Rosalyn's brother. But when Rosalyn tried to talk to her brother about her sister-in-law's behavior, the result, she said, was "shoot the messenger." Rosalyn's brother did not want to discuss her concerns.

So, worried about her niece, Rosalyn called Lovefraud. What should she do?

Father in denial

Rosalyn told me more that makes me think that her concerns

are legitimate — details that I am not including in this article. It also sounds like her brother is a caring man who is in denial or under his wife's control.

Many of us have had to stand by helplessly as someone we cared about was being manipulated by a sociopath. And many of us were that person being manipulated, while our friends and families tried to talk sense into us. The hard reality is that, until someone involved with a sociopath is ready to see what is going on and take steps to leave, there is very little others can do. That appears to be the situation with Rosalyn's brother.

Call the authorities?

Rosalyn asked if she should call the authorities. As heartbreaking as it is, the answer may be no.

Rosalyn is not operating a licensed daycare facility — if she were, she would be legally mandated to report any suspected child abuse. Rosalyn is simply babysitting her niece regularly.

Rosalyn does not have proof that her sister-in-law is harming the child. So if she called the authorities, it would probably backfire. First of all, the sister-in-law works in a profession that most people would find to be incongruous with child abuse. Secondly, her brother does not see, or at least admit to, a problem.

This is a married couple that is living together. If the child doesn't "remember" how she got hurt, the mother denies any wrongdoing, and the father says there is no problem, it is unlikely that Rosalyn will be believed.

Resist the temptation to disparage

Rosalyn asked if she should "plant seeds" in her brother's mind that there might be something wrong with his wife. Again, this is very risky. Here's what Dr. Leedom wrote in a previous blog post, *ASK DR. LEEDOM: How can I get my _____ away from the psychopathic con artist?*

The sociopath will set up situations that narrow, yet intensify, the range of emotions your loved one feels. Be as much of a source of warmth and encouragement that you can. Try to resist any temptation to disparage the sociopath. The responsibility for recognizing the evil in the sociopath has to come from the person him or herself. If the person complains about his/her life, do not react emotionally, instead be a good listener and point out the feelings you see. If you become angry and say to the effect, "How dare he/she treat you this way!" You will see your loved one defend the sociopath, and make you shoulder the emotions he/she should be having about the situation. Instead, your loved one has to personally own all the negative feelings about the sociopath.

Rosalyn's brother is still in the fog, that place of confusion created by the sociopath. Suppose Rosalyn had a "heart-to-heart" with her brother, accusing his wife of child abuse. Suppose the brother then confronted his wife. The woman would convincingly deny any wrongdoing, and then convincingly attack Rosalyn, forbidding the child to ever see Rosalyn again.

Maintain contact with the child

This would be the worst thing that could happen. At least, with Rosalyn, the little girl is safe and happy. She gets a respite from whatever may be going on at home. So the most important thing is for Rosalyn to maintain a connection with the child.

It may be best for Rosalyn to take no direct action to contact authorities, warn the brother or confront the sister-in-law. Instead, it may be best for Rosalyn to bite her tongue, keep her eyes open and make sure she can keep babysitting the little girl.

Rosalyn, should, however document everything that happens. She should keep careful records of any behavior the child exhibits that might point to a problem, photograph any unexplained injuries and videotape the child's acting out.

By doing that, Rosalyn may accumulate evidence for when the child gets old enough to say what is happening to her, or the brother begins to come out of the fog, or the mother screws up — which she will. Then, her documentation may help free the child from an unhappy situation.

When you discover the appalling truth, do not confront the sociopath

You've felt like something was off about your romantic partner for a long time, but you could never quite figure out what it was. Then, suddenly and harshly, you learn the truth.

You discover that this person is cheating on you. Or forged your signature to open up credit cards. Or has kids you never knew about. Or is only pretending to go to work every day. Or is married to someone else.

However it happened, you learn that your partner is betraying you. Your first instinct is to confront your partner and demand answers.

DON'T DO IT.

When you learn what is really going on, the best thing you can do is nothing, at least temporarily. Do not lash out. Instead, no matter how angry and hurt you are, pretend that nothing has changed.

Why? Because when sociopaths know the jig is up, they engage in all kinds of destructive behavior. They may:

- Talk circles around you, convincing you that you are wrong
- Wipe out joint checking accounts or steal any remaining assets
- Destroy evidence you need, such as documents and computer files
- Launch or intensify a smear campaign against you

- Cry crocodile tears in an effort to appeal to your sympathy
- Fly into a rage and destroy your property
- Fabricate criminal charges, such as accusing you of domestic violence
- Claim that you are insane and try to commit you to a mental institution
- Engage in physical violence, injuring you, your children and/or your animals
- Disappear, taking your money or property with them
- Drop all pretense of being your sweet romantic partner, and turn blatantly miserable, cruel and vindictive

So do not react. What you need to do now is gather more information and think about your next move. It's best to do this while the sociopath doesn't know that you know the truth.

The bottom line is that if you're involved with a sociopath, the only reasonable thing to do is extricate yourself from the relationship. But doing that safely, while protecting your assets, family and property, may require planning. You may need to:

- Move your money into new bank accounts that the sociopath can't access
- Make plans to move out, preferably when the sociopath isn't around
- Go to the police and/or find a lawyer
- Make copies of important documents, such as mortgages and deeds, health insurance info and credit card statements
- Gradually move valuables to a safe location
- Back up computers and hard drives
- Line up friends or family members to help you

Learning the shocking truth of the sociopath's behavior is a game-changer. You were always part of a game that the sociopath was playing, but you didn't know it. Now you do.

Right now, you have an advantage — the sociopath doesn't know that you know. Maintain that advantage as long as you can.

Heartbreak and heroism in dealing with child abuse

Damon Moelter, age 16, stood at the lectern of the Battered Mothers Custody Conference and stated that he escaped his abusive father not because he was protected by the family court system, nor because he beat the system. He escaped because he found a way around it.

How? Two weeks earlier, Damon got married. Once he was married, he was emancipated, and his father could no longer demand custody.

As I listened to this young man speak at the conference, which took place last Friday and Saturday at the George Washington University Law School in Washington, D.C., I was on the verge of tears — as were the 100 or so women (and a few men) in the audience. This young man began describing incidents at age 6 that sounded like he was being sexually abused by his father. His mother reported the abuse. A multitude of professionals in the court system from judges to therapists did not believe Damon, and failed to protect him.

The case was a 10-year nightmare, and I invite you to visit a website, SavingDamon.com, that tells the whole story. The first thing you'll see is a TV news video about Damon's wedding. Also, take a look at the supporting documents — the story is an outrage, and the fact that the family court made it worse is even more of an outrage.

Now Damon is free. He living with his mom and looking forward to going back to high school. (The marriage is only on paper.) What struck me about Damon was how incredibly poised he was — the kid is a natural public speaker. He talked eloquently about how his mother worked so hard to protect him, and how her love and efforts saved his life.

And he wasn't the only one to express those sentiments.

More mothers and grown children

At one of the conference events, two mothers who struggled mightily to protect their children demonstrated that children who were once abused can recover to grow up whole and healthy. Dr. Keyaunoosh Kassauei appeared with her son, Zach, who will soon graduate from high school. He cheerfully and enthusiastically talked about his life. Zach played varsity tennis and founded an organization to promote wellness. He plans to pursue a career in medicine.

April Meyer also lost custody of her daughter, Mandy, to her abusive ex-husband. She fled with her daughter and went into hiding to keep her child safe. Then April was caught and went to jail. Mandy was returned to her father, but ran away.

Children of the Underground

Mandy is now in her 20s. She graduated high school and college, and works for a Child Protective Services organization. Because of her own experience dealing with CPS and testifying in court, she knows exactly what her young clients are going through.

Mandy appeared at the conference via Skype, because she and her husband just had their first child. (April, the new grandmother, was ecstatic.) With tears of gratitude, Mandy praised her mother's efforts to protect her. Even when April wasn't totally successful, Mandy knew that her mother loved her and was trying as hard as she could.

Power of love

All of these mothers and their now-grown children talked about their unbreakable love for each other. Even with the abuse they suffered, and despite the callous treatment by American family courts, they endured. Their love kept them going, until one way or another, the abuser no longer had influence over them.

Mothers at the conference who were still in the throes of battle took heart. They saw that maybe if they could hang in, eventually the difficult battle would end.

How the messages we hear all our lives keep us vulnerable to sociopaths

Lovefraud received the following email from a woman who signed it "Tired of Being Targeted."

> My son's wife sends me nasty text messages and leaves insulting voice messages. Then she complains to her husband I'm being rude and disrespectful to her. It's crazy making and she's clearly projecting.
>
> In the past I took the high road and didn't tell him — but all it got me was year after year of estrangement from my son. With nobody to speak in my defense and expose the truth and her unfounded slander habit, I finally decided to send him a long letter and copy him on all her text messages. I'm now waiting to see if he'll respond. Even with the facts squarely in front of him, I realize he might still go along to get along with his wife.
>
> Why is it so many younger people lack good reasoning skills? Why is it people tend to believe the first thing they're told? Mark Twain once said something about it being easier to deceive somebody than to convince them they've been deceived. Perhaps you could write an article so others can benefit from understanding "projecting" and "crazymaking."
>
> I just got tired of pussyfooting around nice. It seemed to me the more I ignored her bad behavior, the more I became a target. There's a therapist who said he was so tired of ther-

apists making excuses for people's bad behavior, such as them having a bad childhood or something. He said some people who came from a bad environment grew up to be good people. Some who grew up privileged grew up to be bad people. He mentioned something about shaming these people calling them out on their bad behavior.

One of the reasons I sent my son the email was because I was tired of being targeted by evil people and didn't want my daughter-in-law piggyback on my ex-husband's slander. My son (an engineer so it's understandable) is a "true believer" — he stopped thinking early on and is committed to faulty beliefs and any new facts are not brought to bear. I like to call this "lazy brain syndrome." You can quote me on that, too.

I can tell you stories about my gaslighting ex you wouldn't believe. Looking back I realize I was so gullible! It would have been nice if somebody sat me down and explained to me how I should listen to that little voice inside of me that says, "Something ain't right here and why am I now in Kansas?"

Tired of Being Targeted

Donna Andersen responds

Dear Tired,

First of all, I am sorry for what you have endured from your daughter-in-law, and I can understand why you are Tired of Being Targeted.

You asked, "Why is it so many younger people lack good reasoning skills? Why is it people tend to believe the first thing they're told?"

When it comes to recognizing and understanding sociopathic behavior, I'm afraid that the problem is much more complex than poor reasoning skills. The way I see it, there are three major failures in society that enable sociopaths to engage in, and get away with, their atrocious behavior:

- We don't know that sociopaths exist.

- We don't understand psychological manipulation.
- We aren't taught to use the one tool that can protect us.

Clueless about sociopaths

As many as 40 million adults in the United States may have exploitative personality disorders — antisocial, narcissistic, borderline or histrionic. These are the people I refer to as "sociopaths." Most of us don't know they exist.

In 2011, the scientific journal, Innovations in Clinical Neuroscience, published an article that examined previous studies of the prevalence of personality disorders in the United States and around the world. The authors examined five American and four international studies, dating back to 1989, and the studies consistently showed that about 10% of the general population have personality disorders.

The most recent U.S. study is the scariest. It found the following percentages of exploitative personality disorders among non-institutionalized people aged 18 and older:

Antisocial personality disorder — 3.8%
Borderline personality disorder — 5.9%
Narcissistic personality disorder — 6.2%
Histrionic personality disorder — 1.8%

These are the people who live their lives by exploiting and manipulating others. Add them up and it's 17.7% of the adult U.S. population, or about 40 million adults.

So 40 million people go through life taking advantage of us, and most of us don't know they exist. How does this happen?

Cultural myths that blind us to danger

All our lives, we hear cultural messages in church, school and the media, like the following:

- "We're all created equal."

- "We all just want to be loved."
- "Everybody has good inside."

Unfortunately, these statements are not true for everybody. They are true for the approximately 82% of the population who are capable of normal love and empathy. The statements are not true for the approximately 18% of the population who have anti-social, narcissistic, borderline or histrionic personality disorders.

No one tells us that there are exceptions to these feel-good maxims. No one tells us that human predators live among us, and that we need to protect ourselves from them.

In fact, we hear messages that put us in even more danger, like:

- "Everyone deserves a second chance."
- "Give him/her the benefit of the doubt."
- "We all have issues/problems/flaws."

The bottom line: We don't know that we are surrounded by personality-disordered people who want to take advantage of us. And when we do experience or witness bad behavior, we're told to explain it away.

Psychological manipulation

All of this sets us up for psychological manipulation by the sociopaths.

Human beings are social animals, and our survival as a species was assured over the millennia because we developed the ability to trust each other. Trust is built into our DNA.

When sociopaths target us for manipulation, the first step is taking advantage of our trust. They use love bombing, deception and the pity play to reel us in. Once we are hooked, they increase the psychological pressure through tactics like information control, gaslighting and intermittent reinforcement.

We may eventually suspect that something is not right in our relationship. But this can lead to cognitive dissonance, which is the mental stress of holding two conflicting beliefs at the same time, or the discomfort of being presented with facts that conflict with our beliefs. When this happens, many of us dump the facts in order to keep the beliefs.

So what happens? The sociopath keeps the pressure up, and psychological bond we feel with him or her becomes stronger and stronger. In time, we can lose our "agency," which is the capacity to act independently and make our own decisions. That's why it is so hard to break free of the exploiter.

Listening to the inner voice

Tired, you are right in that the answer for all of us is to learn to listen to our inner voice. Our intuition also developed over the millennia, and its purpose is to warn us about predators.

And what cultural messages do we receive about intuition? None! In fact, instinct is pooh-poohed. We learn that we're supposed to be rational, and make judgments based on evidence and proof, not on a gut feeling.

Anyway, given society's general cluelessness about sociopaths and manipulation, I would guess that your son may need more than better reasoning skills to see what is really going on. For him, recognizing the truth of his wife's behavior and how it is affecting you may entail:

- Understanding that sociopaths exist, and they are everywhere
- Believing that his wife is targeting you for no reason
- Overcoming cognitive dissonance the woman he married is engaged in mean-spirited behavior towards his mother
- Accepting that his wife is disordered will not change

This is the path all of us have traveled in order to escape the sociopaths in our lives and make amends to the people we have hurt. It's a very difficult journey.

Cultural conspiracy?

But let's get back to the big picture of our cultural messages:

We are surrounded by millions of predators, but no one tells us about them.

We are encouraged to trust everyone, including the predators.

We are discouraged from listening to our intuition, which protects us from predators.

I'd hate to think of a massive conspiracy, but it seems to me that our culture is set up to make us vulnerable to sociopaths.

Do we really just stand by and let these people hurt others?

Last week I heard from a woman who realized that her work supervisor was probably disordered.

The Lovefraud reader was hired by a school system to work one-on-one with a special needs child, but what she was directed to do made no sense. When she asked the school district's "professionals" about the "therapy," since, in her experience, it was inappropriate for the child's needs, they seemed uncomfortable and never really answered her. The supervisor, in the meantime, became belligerent. The Lovefraud reader saw that the supervisor was controlling, the professionals were intimidated, and the child was not receiving the right care.

The Lovefraud reader was so upset that she took medical leave, and the supervisor asked her to resign. She is now unemployed.

After describing the experience, our Lovefraud reader asked: "Do we really just stand by and let these people hurt children, innocent disabled children, workers underneath them, and look the other way?"

Aggressive personalities

This is the most frustrating and disheartening aspect of learning what sociopaths are: Now we can identify them. We know what they are doing. We know that whomever they are doing it to will be damaged. And we feel like we can't stop the exploiters.

Sociopaths, through charm, deceit and ruthlessness, ensconce themselves in positions of power, whether it's in a work environment, an organization, a social network or a family. Their objective is to maintain power and control.

Dr. George K. Simon explains this in his book, *Character Disturbance*. He writes:

> Aggressive personalities strive for the dominant position at all times and in all circumstances. This premise is very hard for the average person, especially the neurotic individual, to understand, let alone accept. It's incomprehensible for most of us to conceive that in every situation, every encounter, every engagement, the aggressive personality is predisposed to jockey with us for the superior position, even in situations with no recognizable need to do so. The failure to understand and accept this, however, is how aggressive personalities so often succeed in their quest to gain advantage over others.

Sociopaths manipulate their way into dominant positions, and then continue to manipulate in order to stay there. The longer they are in these dominant positions, the more power they accumulate, and the less others are willing to go up against them.

And then we come along, perceive the dynamic, see the damage, and want to do something about it.

Understand the reality

I am all for exposing sociopaths in any way possible. I want to hold them accountable. I want justice for the people they victimize. I want to prevent them from hurting anyone else. But before I suggest that you take any action, I want to make sure you understand what you are dealing with. Here are some points to keep in mind:

1. Sociopaths are ruthless in pursuit of their objective. They will cajole, lie, cheat or bully — whatever gets them what they want. They do not care about following the rules, protocol or even the law. If sociopaths decide it's more convenient to stay within

the law, they may go right to the edge but not break it. Sociopaths are experts at operating in the gray areas.

2. People around the sociopath are likely already compromised. The sociopath has probably lined up allies, or at least people who are afraid to go against him or her. These people have been brown-nosed, bought off or intimidated.

3. You may already be compromised. If a sociopath is preparing to discard you, or perceives you as a threat, he or she may have launched a smear campaign, convincingly expressing concern about your behavior or mental stability to everyone you know. By the time you approach them with your concerns, they are primed to discount whatever you say.

4. The authorities may not act. Unless a law has clearly been broken, the police won't do anything. And unless a case can be proven and won in court, a prosecutor won't file charges. Also, whether law enforcement or any other authority decides to look into a matter may depend on the organization's politics.

5. Sociopaths relish confrontation, and view it as a game to win. Even if you manage to get the person in court or some other arbitration venue, he or she will put on an incredible performance — using tears, righteous indignation, whatever — in order to come out on top. They are very, very good at it.

You come first

This is all really depressing. Do we really just stand by watching sociopaths run rampant, from one victim to the next?

Here's the most important thing to keep in mind when contemplating exposing a sociopath: Your first responsibility is to yourself.

Are you in a position of strength? Your physical safety is most important, but you also need to be concerned about your financial, reputational and legal safety. When the sociopath counterattacks, which he or she will do, can you withstand it?

If you can't engage a sociopath head-on, can you do anything covertly? Perhaps you can quietly tell people what the sociopath is really like, and let word-of-mouth take over.

If you decide to take on the sociopath, you'll need two things: irrefutable evidence of the sociopath's behavior, and nerves of steel. Many Lovefraud readers have no choice but to face the sociopath in court. If you do, you'll need to stay calm, collected and professional at all times. The sociopath will most likely try to get an emotional reaction out of you. Do not react — it's like feeding the beast.

Spread the word

Perhaps it's too dangerous for you to try to expose the particular sociopath that you tangled with. It doesn't mean you have to stay totally silent on the subject.

Whenever an opportunity arises, teach people the basic truths about sociopaths: They exist, and they are destructive. Learn the signs of sociopathic behavior and explain them to others. If we raise the general awareness of these predators, there will be fewer people for them to victimize.

Psychopaths as puppet masters

You and I feel personal satisfaction through accomplishment, or warm human relationships, or being of service to others.

Psychopaths feel personal satisfaction through pulling the so-called strings and making people jump.

They do something that they know will upset you just to see you cry. They trap you into no-win situations to watch you squirm. They devalue and discard you, so they can watch you fall apart.

Why do they do this?

Social motivations

The answer lies at the heart of the personality disorder. According to Dr. Liane Leedom, psychopaths have an out-of-control power motivation.

Researchers have identified four social motivations. These are basic motivations that people, as social animals, have regarding other people. They are:

- Attachment — desire to be with other people, especially mates, family and tribe
- Sex — for enjoyment, bonding and reproduction
- Caregiving — doing what is best for other people's health and wellbeing
- Power — desire for higher rank and privilege

Anyone can have these motivations to greater or lesser degrees. In most people, the social motivations balance each other out. For example, the power motivation makes people want to achieve and be leaders, so it isn't necessarily bad. Usually, the attachment and caregiving motivations keep it in check. Most people are willing to go after what they want, but don't want to harm other people in the process.

Psychopaths are different

Psychopaths feel the attachment motivation — they want to be with other people. They certainly want sex. And they really want power.

They do not, however, experience the caregiving motivation. Psychopaths are really only interested in themselves, and have no concern at all about the welfare of others. (If they seem to be displaying concern, it's only because they have an ulterior motive.)

The bottom line, then, is that psychopaths have a really strong power motivation, and no caregiving motivation to put the brakes on it. So what they really want in life is power and control.

Yes, they want sex, but they want power and control more. Psychopaths aren't necessarily sex-crazed fiends. Many either engage in sex — or withhold it — in order to increase their power and control.

Do NOT react

Psychopaths love being the puppet master — making other people react feeds their desire for power and control.

That's why No Contact is so important. No Contact changes the dynamic. It takes you out of the psychopath's feedback loop, because they can't get their power-and-control fix.

If No Contact is not possible, or not possible yet, the next best strategy is DO NOT react. When psychopaths try to provoke you, do not respond emotionally — at least in front of them. Even if you have to temporarily be the world's greatest actress or actor, do not let them know that they've upset you.

If you can keep this up, hopefully the psychopath will get bored and lose interest in you. When you don't react, you're no fun anymore.

The idea is to cut the puppet master strings, so that you can achieve your freedom.

Does he sound like a full-blown narcissist and/or sociopath?

Editor's note: Lovefraud received the following letter from a reader whom we'll call "bonnie2017." Donna Andersen responds to her questions at the end of the letter. Names have been changed.

Following my most recent life-shattering break-up 4 weeks ago, I happened upon your website, lovefraud.com, and found it extremely helpful and insightful! I first wanted to thank you for all the invaluable information you provide. I also wanted to tell you my sad story about my almost-baby-daddy and get your feedback. Maybe it can help others too.

From January through May, I had been unknowingly dating what I thought was a narcissist (but recently realized he may actually be a sociopath?). From the beginning, he was intoxicating: 30-years old, tall (6'4"), extremely handsome, athletic, sharp, intelligent, confident, nice, up for anything.

It was an explosive and exciting courtship, during which he love-bombed my phone all day every day with "good morning beautiful" and frequent heart emojis texts. He told me how I was "different from other women" and how "he's never been this attracted to" or "this excited about" someone before.

He was taking me out on real dinner dates (so rare

Does he sound like a full-blown narcissist and/or sociopath?

these days) and even bought me flowers (tulips, my favorite!). His affection was intoxicating and almost oppressive, as I found myself swept up in an immediate romantic (and passionately sexual) relationship with a man I barely knew.

Something off

Despite our instant attraction and connection, there was something off about him, a sad darkness in his eyes and a stare that was deeply penetrating (he rarely blinked), even innocently childish.

Things seemed to revolve around him and his needs... but I was able to ignore the negative aspects because of our apparent shared family and political values, our stimulating intellectual conversations and our insanely amazing sexual chemistry (high levels of testosterone) - the makings of a once-in-a-lifetime type of relationship, right?!

About 8 weeks in, I got scared of the fury of the pace and pulled back. My instincts were kicking in, and although he assured me that he was "definitely not seeing anyone else" and wanted "only to be with me," I had this nagging feeling that he was playing me, or worse, that something was deeply off.

He did not react well to my distancing act, and he promptly turned on me. When I asked him if we could "slow things down," he became immediately colder, began withholding affection from me, gave me silent treatments...like he was punishing me. He still texted every day, but not like before; he was tossing me crumbs.

Feelings and emotions were off-limits, though his sexual desire and expectations remained fierce, almost animalistic. I tried for several weeks to get the sweetness and fireworks back again, but to no avail.

Last straw

The last straw was one night, after hours of talking in circles about the relationship, he sat pouting with his arms crossed in front of him, and said frighteningly: "I feel dead

179

inside." Yikes! I ended it then and there.

Looking back on this part of our relationship, I can see that he was actually quite dull, almost an empty shell that thrived on outside proposals and excitement. He would say weird things about himself and past relationships that were almost like warnings, like "I can be really moody" and that he has "rarely lived in the same city as anyone he's dated."

He also told me on several occasions that he "didn't know what he wanted" with anything, and that he has been that way for as long as he can remember. He was very unhappy in his job as an English teacher and felt very unfulfilled, but didn't know what else to do with his life.

He didn't have many male friends, only his friends from back home with whom he would play online video games most nights. He had one long-term girlfriend for whom he actually moved across several states, but when she wanted to take the next step and get married, he broke up with her. He seemed to have zero attachment to her or to previous girlfriends, whom he implied were usually "too needy" or "wanted to sink their claws in."

He liked me because I was so "cool" and didn't act jealous or ask too many questions about his routines (he is a former college athlete and now obsessed with the gym and with his appearance). He said he didn't have a type, but usually dated women who were a bit older and who had "cool stuff going on" in their lives.

His default seemed to be "I don't care." He even told me that he is usually always single and lonely and that he chooses not to care because it's "easier."

Anyway, 4 weeks after the first break-up, we got back in touch organically. A text message here and there. He had lent me one of his books to read, so we decided to meet up, catch up and return his book.

I'm pregnant

The next day, I found out I was pregnant. Major panic!! My first reaction was to terminate, though it wasn't my true desire. I decided to tell him before making a decision.

Dreading it, I showed up to his house, he greeted me kindly, and we went inside for a visit. I struggled to tell him and couldn't hold back the tears.

And POOF! Upon hearing the words "I'm pregnant" he catapulted back into superhero, perfect romantic love-bomb man! He came to me, hugged and kissed me tenderly and said, "I support you in every way"... he was excited and passionate again, talking about his extreme attraction to me, the ideal woman carrying his child.

He told me we could get back together, have a baby and a perfect beautiful family. He started trying to convince me of the wonderful life we could have with him as the ultimate provider: he owned his own home, had a good job with insurance, his parents would relocate and help us with the baby. He told me I was the most amazing woman he'd ever met and we should never have broken up in the first place, we could even get married, etc. He even told me that having a baby would "force him to grow up" (double yikes!).

I was completely sucked in again - my big, strong, paternal he-man had come to my rescue! Then, when he assured me he had not seen ANYONE since we broke up 5 weeks before, we had INCREDIBLY passionate (and *unprotected*) sex that night...and almost every night after for the next 5 weeks.

More distant

As we started to research about parenting and insurance and marriage and all the scary gown-up things, he slowly became more and more distant. He would turn things around on me and go back on promises. He started making decisions without me, and when I would confront him, he would deny it or ignore me.

He blew hot and cold... one minute he was going to ultrasound appointments with me and saying "I'd love to be a dad with you" and "I'm going to spoil my baby mama rotten" and the next it was "we shouldn't jump back into this relationship, we barely know each other"...

When I told him it was okay if he wanted to break-up and not deal with it, he angrily accused me of "trying to push him away." He would party with his 2 or 3 friends all day and night, then come back to me and insist we go to counseling together because this was all "so hard on him." I was going insane and falling apart, knowing in my heart that I could not go through with having his baby.

Sad day

After a 3-day angry silent treatment from my baby daddy-to-be (because I didn't come over when he wanted) and some very deep introspection, I finally made the excruciatingly difficult decision to terminate the pregnancy. He had gone from supportive and loving superdad to completely cold and detached in a span of 2 weeks.

On the sad day, he was "there" for me, he took me to the appointment and he brought me food and ice cream afterwards... but he wasn't really there.

I was devastated. A complete emotional, physical and spiritual wreck. He disappeared for several days. When I needed him most.

Then he resurfaced, quite half-assedly. He told me all the same non-committal things as before, that he "cared for me but still didn't know what he wanted" and that he was "immature" and couldn't have a real relationship with me. He said it was "painful for him to see me" cause it reminded him of our loss. I realized I couldn't really count on him as a partner, but I didn't want to lose him completely, after all we'd been through.

Can we be friends?

In my heart, I thought he was a good man, but maybe not the right man for me. I knew he had some major emotional issues and was struggling with all of this, and I didn't want him to suffer.

On our next date night, he took me out for dinner and ice cream. When he wanted me to come home with him, I told him I'd been on a date with someone else and asked him if we could be friends.

Well, he LOST IT and became extremely aggressive (later through text), saying that he had been "so faithful to me" and that he had "put his entire dating life on hold" out of respect for me and because he wanted to "do right by me and the baby." He was so pissed that I was "deceiving" him by making him think I still wanted to be with him, and he said if he'd known I was seeing other people, he never would have made such a valiant effort to keep a relationship going with me.

He said he "didn't care who I dated, but that I should be honest with him." Then he switched to "there's no way we could be just friends" because I would always be "the mother of his child" in his mind. He said we had the best sex, and that it was because we had an emotional connection (something I believe he rarely has with women). He said he still cared for me and didn't think we'd gotten a real chance to "figure us out yet."

Well, I felt terrible and agreed to give it one more chance. We went home to our respective places.

Other women

That same night he called his side piece, Brittany, and she went over to his place at 10:30 pm to have sex with him.

On our next date night two nights later, after a great romantic love-filled evening (including more unprotected sex), I checked his phone while he was sleeping.

Sure enough, he had been having sex with Brittany (and one or two other women) on and off THE ENTIRE TIME I WAS PREGNANT. The entire time he was trying to convince me to marry him and have his perfect child. The whole time I was recovering from a traumatic loss and painful surgery. The day after the abortion, while I was lying in bed crying and bleeding, he went to a baseball game with her. He even made my sweet potato recipe for her one night while I was with my sister!

I woke him up at 5 am and asked him calmly, "Have you been seeing other people?"

He replied, "No."

I said, "Really? Are you sure? I don't think you're being honest with me."

He continued lying... "No, we've talked about this 100 times."

I said, "Then who is Brittany?"

He said, "She's a friend."

I picked up his phone, and I said, "I just saw in here that she is not a friend."

Silence ... Then he finally said, "well I guess you already know then."

I said, "The whole time I was pregnant...why would do that to me?"

He said, "Because I'm a shitty person."

I said, "Why did you get angry with me for wanting to move on, and profess to be some great man who stood honorably by me?"

He said again, coldly, "Because I'm a really terrible person."

He proceeded to tell me that he had "helped" me, when he didn't have to.

On the brink of a full-blown panic attack, I got up and I and left. He followed me to the door and did not say a word.

We have not spoken in 4 weeks, he has never apologized or attempted to contact me directly since.

I immediately went to the clinic for an STD test (all negative, thank god). I have deleted him from my phone and social media sites. He still stalks my social media pages and watches everything I do.

Questions

It is so difficult to get closure and clarity on this experience, and I would love to have your objective opinion and advice on several points:

- Why is he still checking in on me?
- If he ever cared, why would he lie to my face so callously?
- Why did he drag out my pregnancy and pretend to be the perfect dad?
- Why do I still feel so emotionally attached to this terrible toxic person?
- Does he sound like a full-blown narcissist and/or sociopath? Or maybe some form of borderline personality disorder?

Even after all this, I don't feel that he purposefully hurts people. I think he just does what he wants, and when shit goes wrong, he withdraws back into his safe "I don't care" place.

He fits MANY of the descriptions on the sociopath checklist: lying, cheating, easily bored, dead eyes, empty inside, self-obsessed, shallow, immature, lack of remorse, lack of long-term goals, trouble with empathy... but there are many that he doesn't have.

He is very close to his family, he has a strong sense of "taking responsibility for one's actions," he does not seem to lie just for the sake of lying and I have seen flashes of compassion and empathy in him. But he is a liar, so everything he says is probably complete garbage.

Thank you for your insight during this extremely painful and heartbreaking time.

Donna Andersen responds

Bonnie2017, I am so sorry for your experience. The mind games with this man were bad, the cheating was worse, and having to decide to terminate the pregnancy was horrible.

Still, I support your decision. Having a child with a sociopath is a nightmare. One of two things would have happened. Either he would have abandoned you to take care of the child on your own (even if you were still together), or he would have used the child as a pawn to control and even torment you for the rest of your life.

To make matters worse, these personality disorders are highly genetic. So there is a chance that your child would have inherited a predisposition to a personality disorder, which parenting may or may not be able to overcome. Having made your choice, you'll be able to recover, move on, and create the type of life that you want.

Here are my responses to your questions:

1. Why is he still checking in on me?

We never really know why sociopaths do anything, but I can think of a few potential reasons why he is stalking your social media.

First, sociopaths typically equate relationship with ownership, and view their partners as their property. This is especially true when children are involved. Even though you have broken up, he probably still views you as his property, and he wants to know what his property is doing.

Second, sociopaths are all about power and control. He may be looking for an opportunity to exert power and control over you again. You ended the involvement with him (good for you!). I've heard stories of sociopaths who, after a breakup, reeled their former partners back in, promising the world, acting on their best behavior until the partner believes they truly have changed — just so the sociopaths can be the ones to dump the partner.

Third, sociopaths often keep track of former partners just in case they want to use them again. From a sociopathic point of view, they were able to exploit you once, so they assume they'll be able to exploit you again.

The key for you is to maintain No Contact. If he tries to get in touch with you again, ignore him.

2. If he ever cared, why would he lie to my face so callously?

Here's what you need to understand: Sociopaths do not have the ability to love. Let me explain.

Researchers have found that there are three parts necessary for true romantic love:

- Attachment — this is the desire to be with someone to whom you are attracted.
- Sex — the desire for physical intimacy and procreation.
- Caregiving — this is the desire to take care of, and do what is best for, the people for whom you feel love.

All three parts are necessary for real love.

Now, sociopaths can do the first two parts. They want attachment and sex. But they cannot do caregiving. They do not truly care about anybody but themselves. They cannot put someone else's interests before their own.

Sometimes they can appear to be caregiving, but there is always an agenda. If sociopaths are taking care of someone, it is to butter them up for later exploitation.

So unfortunately, your first statement is not true. He never truly cared for you. And because of that, it was easy for him to lie to you.

3. Why did he drag out my pregnancy and pretend to be the perfect dad?

Again, it's hard to know the exact reason why, but I can make a few guesses.

Novelty. Sociopaths love novelty, and if he doesn't have a child, he may look at it as something that he hasn't done before. Many sociopaths like playing with their new babies; to them, it's like playing with a new toy. They may like the fun parts of having kids, but they are not interested in the hard work of childrearing. Or, they lose interest all together.

Image. Sociopaths often want a spouse and kids because that's the type of image they want in the community. Some sociopaths start a family so that they appear to be upstanding citizens — perfect cover if they want to live a double life.

Power and control. Sociopaths know that having a child with someone ties them together forever. It's the ultimate power and control.

4. Why do I still feel so emotionally attached to this terrible toxic person?

Involvements with sociopaths are highly addictive. Sociopaths hijack the human bonding system, so the normal psychological and biological aspects of romantic relationships are stronger than ever. All of these factors are especially true in your case because of your pregnancy, and your decision to terminate.

The answer is to break the addiction by having No Contact with this man. Eventually, the attachment will dissipate.

5. Does he sound like a full-blown narcissist and/or sociopath? Or maybe some form of borderline personality disorder?

The distinctions between these disorders are not clear. In fact, "sociopath" is no longer a clinical term.

Lovefraud uses the word "sociopath" as an umbrella term for all manipulative and exploitative personality disorders: Antisocial, narcissistic, borderline personality disorders and psychopathy.

Disordered individuals are not all the same. Multiple traits make up these disorders, and it is possible to have some traits and not the others. Additionally, an individual can have any of the traits to greater or lesser degrees. In the end, even experts often have difficulty making a diagnosis.

The bottom line is that it doesn't matter. The man is definitely disordered, he is toxic, and he will never change.

I am glad that you got away from him. Now, give yourself time and permission to recover. I assure you, you can get past this experience.

To get rid of a sociopath, think out of the box!

One way to convince a sociopath to leave you alone may be to make yourself unappealing. Here are suggestions from a Lovefraud reader:

> Why all the drama with the cops, probation, looking over shoulder, parole, etc.? The secret seems to be getting the stalker to want no further parts of you. My cousin did that by explaining an elective surgery as a bowel surgery and with a product called Liquid Ass sprayed down the back of her pants confronted him outside her house with the explanation that it's a lifelong after effect she'll have to live with. This sociopath was a daily threat and annoyance and that was the last time she ever saw him, which was August of 2011. Horrid stench along with whatever else would be the last thing the particular stalker would ever want is what she has to become until he's gone. He doesn't like overweight women? Grab a fork! Do the lovelies get a copy of the victim impact statement before the parole board? Buy lots and lots of guns, assault rifles, rocket launcher and go on about them in the statement ... That you don't think he deserves capital punishment and she doesn't want to be forced to administer it in her own house. It's crazy outside the box thinking but it works.

3 tips for polite conversation about relationship abuse

I recently attended a small party — about 15 people — at a friend's home. I got into a conversation with two women, neither of whom I knew before. They both revealed that, like me, they had endured relationship abuse. We started swapping stories.

The first woman worked hard all her life, built a successful career, and then married the guy who, over about seven years, took advantage of her assets. She described his lies, mostly about money, as "gaslighting."

The second woman had three children with a man who turned out to be a controller, moving her away from family and friends. She spent 20 years trying to shield the children from his destructive ways, then finally divorced him.

I was amazed. Years ago, when I first launched Lovefraud, no one talked about relationship abuse. Now, people are familiar with terms like "gaslighting" and "narcissist." Discussion of relationship abuse has gone mainstream — it's now an acceptable topic of conversation at social events.

This is terrific progress, because:

- The best way to deal with relationship abuse is to avoid it.
- The best way to avoid relationship abuse is to know it exists.
- And the best way to know relationship abuse exists is to talk about it.

3 tips for polite conversation about relationship abuse

So, how do you have a polite conversation about relationship abuse? Here are some tips:

First, focus on your own recovery

If you are still feeling traumatized about your experience, it's fine to talk about what happened to you with a competent therapist, or someone who shares your experience. But it may be premature to talk about it to a casual acquaintance, or even friends and family.

Why? Because many people have difficulty listening to stories of relationship abuse. As Dr. Karin Huffer explained, protective filters kick in. "If an individual begins to share with another and the data threatens the listener's feelings of safety," she says, "they may try to divert the data or simply not hear it at all."

Much human communication is nonverbal — it's tone of voice, gestures, body language. When you're still traumatized about what happened, your listeners can sense this — and it scares them. They react to your emotional vibes — and shut out what you are saying.

So before engaging in a casual conversation about your experience, you need to be far enough along your healing journey that you can discuss it calmly. You'll get there. But until then, it's probably best to keep the details vague.

Second, educate yourself about personality disorders and relationship abuse

You've been through the experience. But, from an educational perspective, here are the basic facts:

1. The people who engage in relationship abuse usually have some level of an exploitative personality disorder — antisocial, narcissistic, borderline, histrionic or psychopathic. (Lovefraud groups them together under the umbrella term of "sociopaths.")
2. Approximately 30 million adults in the United States could be diagnosed with one of these disorders. Sociopaths are male and female, all races, all religions

and can be found in all segments of society.

3. Sociopaths target normal people and hijack the human bonding system. At first, they are typically charming, exciting and charismatic. Later, once they have hooked you into a relationship, they become controlling and abusive.

4. Although many people believe sociopaths are serial killers, very few of them actually commit murder. In fact, many sociopaths engage in behavior that is immoral or unethical, but not necessarily illegal.

5. Sociopaths are not delusional. They know exactly what they are doing.

Third, wait for opportunities to talk about relationship abuse

There was a time when relationship abuse simply wasn't mentioned. Times have changed.

The #MeToo movement is drawing attention to sexual assault. TV shows such as Dirty John, Surviving R. Kelly, and Seduced by Evil bring relationship abuse right into your living room. So now, more than ever, the topic is likely to come up in general conversation. When it does, it's an opportunity for you share what you know.

Here's the point that I suggest you make: It can happen to anyone.

People tend to believe that relationship abuse only happens to women with low self-esteem. That's not true. First of all, it happens to both men and women. And secondly, it happens to people who are accomplished, successful and achievement-oriented — and who have a vulnerability. Guess what? We all have vulnerabilities, so we are all potential targets.

Whether you share any of your experience or not — that's totally up to you — you can certainly share your insight. So when an opportunity arises, please keep the conversation going. The more we talk about relationship abuse, raising general awareness of the signs and symptoms, the more others can escape before too much damage is done.

To survive a sociopath, we sometimes act like a sociopath

I almost didn't recognize myself. There I was, plotting with my cheating husband's mistress to steal money from his bank account.

Before I married James Montgomery, I never would have considered such an action. But after he convinced me to blow $227,000 on his ridiculous business schemes, and after I discovered that my entire marriage was a scam, I was angry, broke and desperate. I did what I had to do to survive a sociopath (although at the time, I didn't know he was a sociopath).

Maybe because of your own entanglement with a sociopath, you've found yourself doing things that you never, ever did before. This happened to "Stevie2018," who just posted her story in the Lovefraud Forum. Her boyfriend invited her to spend the night, and while she was there, was texting another woman. She writes:

> I lost it, threw the phone at him, screamed a lot... then went to the garage and broke only the presents I gave him.. ie glasses for Xmas, crystal bowl for Father's Day.

The boyfriend, of course, blamed her for violating his privacy (a typical sociopathic denial strategy). And Stevie2018 says she is embarrassed, because she's never done anything like this in her life.

> I'm ashamed, my self esteem in gone, and now he's telling our friends I trashed his house... which I did not.

Read her entire post, entitled, *Am I the "crazy" one?*, in the Lovefraud Forum.

Reacting to the sociopath

In response to Stevie2018's question, no, no, no, she is not crazy. She also has no reason to feel embarrassed. Stevie2018 was simply reacting to the insanity and betrayal perpetrated by her sociopath boyfriend.

With their deception and manipulation, sociopaths do two things: They break all of the rules of social interaction, and they push us to the limits of our endurance. Whether we face physical danger, financial destruction or a complete loss of self, we reach the point where we must do whatever is necessary to save ourselves.

Sometimes that means bending or even breaking the rules, because we learn that the rules aren't going to help us.

Sometimes it means flying into a rage. After tolerating so much abuse, we either have to release our emotions or self-destruct. We lash out in anger.

Anger, for normal people, is a scary emotion — probably because we have bad memories of being the brunt of someone else's anger. But anger, when warranted, actually protects us. It spurs us into action — such as expelling the sociopath from our lives.

We are not sociopaths

When we do things that are so contrary to our nature, our actions surprise us. We wonder if we have become just as bad as our tormenter.

Yes, our behavior in particular situations may resemble that of a sociopath. But no, we have not turned into a sociopath. We are reacting to the sociopath's provocation. They are at fault, not us.

I would not criticize anyone who has bee targeted by a sociopath and reacts aggressively. However, I will say that sometimes it's a tactical error. I've heard from plenty of people who were so angry that they finally hit the sociopath, and found themselves arrested for domestic violence. I've also heard from people who screamed at the sociopath in anger, only to learn that the sociopath recorded the tirade and used it against them.

Sociopaths can drive us to violate our own standards of behavior, but that does not mean we become sociopaths. How do we know? Because we feel badly about our actions. Sociopaths don't.

The answer is to escape the disordered individual. Once the sociopath is out of our lives and we're on the road to recovery, we will return to our regular selves.

10 lessons on divorcing a sociopath
I learned the hard way

Throughout my marriage to the sociopath, James Montgomery, I was confused. He kept telling me that he loved me, but he went through all my money, put me in debt, and didn't care that I was upset about it. What kind of marriage was that?

When I finally discovered that Montgomery was cheating on me, in fact, that he had a child with another woman during our marriage, my first reaction was relief. Now I could leave.

I wanted this man out of my life as soon as possible, which meant I needed a divorce. Here's what I learned about divorcing a sociopath.

1. When divorcing a sociopath, you need a good attorney

The first attorney I consulted, who was suggested by a friend, was awful. I told him about Montgomery taking all my money, showed him the photos I found of my husband with another woman's child, and he pretty much didn't care.

I then used connections to get a better referral and found a terrific lawyer. She was smart, diligent and willing to stand up for me. It made all the difference in the world.

2. The sociopath will get his/her day in court

When I started the divorce process, I thought it was so obvious that my husband was a con artist who had intentionally stolen my money that the judge would see it right away, order him to pay me back and I would be made whole.

Nope. This is court, where judgment is rendered only after a formal process of reviewing the evidence. I suppose it's a good thing — we all deserve a chance to make our cases. But still, it was a shock to my system, especially when my attorney and I had to practically do cartwheels to keep my husband informed about the process when he obviously couldn't care less.

3. Sociopaths lie — including on court documents

My complaint for divorce was a litany of Montgomery's deceitful and exploitative behavior — and he denied all of it, except for the fact that he had fathered a child with another woman. He might have denied that too, except I had the birth certificate.

In his counter complaint, he accused me of abuse — including that I was violent towards him and I destroyed his property. I was shocked! I have never been violent towards anyone or anything. But sociopaths are pathological liars, even in court.

4. Documentation when divorcing a sociopath is critical

Throughout my entire marriage, Montgomery promised me that he would repay me for all the money I spent trying to help him launch his businesses. So I tracked the expenses as we went along — I used Quicken for my business accounting, so it was easy.

On August 16, 1998, during our one of our frequent arguments about money, I accused him of taking everything I had, and he raged the he would pay me back. I demanded that he put his promise in writing. I was sitting at my desk, so I whipped out a sheet of letterhead, dated it and scrawled by hand:

> James Montgomery agrees to repay Donna Andersen for all the expenses she has paid on his behalf and agrees that he is responsible for all credit card debt.

He signed it. And this document, written in anger and haste, was the critical proof that Montgomery had promised to pay me back.

If you have given your spouse money based on his or her

promises to repay you, you must have this documented in writing. If you don't, it will be very difficult to collect any money.

5. Court orders mean nothing to a sociopath

My attorney followed the typical divorce process: Soon after my complaint for divorce was filed, we filed a motion for temporary support. I spent thousands of dollars on this motion, and the judge granted it.

Montgomery was ordered to pay me about $800 a month while the divorce was underway. He never paid a dime.

6. Sociopaths feel no obligation to comply with court requirements

My husband was supposed to complete an official court form disclose his income and expenditures. When he turned the form in, everything was blank.

Finally, my husband fired his attorney, said he was representing himself, and never showed up for the trial.

7. When divorcing a sociopath, it helps to prove a pattern of conduct

I wasn't my husband's only victim. After I left Montgomery, I started looking through his documents that he left in my home (I had previously avoided them, out of respect for his privacy). I discovered that, before and during our marriage, he'd been involved 20 or 30 other women. Many of them were asking for their money back.

Three of these women, plus the parents of his wife before me who died, testified at my divorce. The money Montgomery took from the five of us totaled more than $1 million.

The testimony of the other women convinced the judge that my marriage wasn't just a relationship gone bad, but that Montgomery intentionally scammed me. In legal jargon, we proved a "pattern of conduct." The judge awarded me all the money that Montgomery took from me — $227,000 — plus $1 million in punitive damages.

8. The court doesn't help you collect your money

The judge signed an order stating that Montgomery owed me more than $1.2 million and was responsible for all credit card debt. Once he signed the order, the judge was finished with the case.

The court had issued a judgment against Montgomery. He was ordered to pay me, but — surprise, surprise — he didn't. Now what?

Well, I was a judgment creditor, and Montgomery was a judgment debtor. That meant that I had to follow all the regular laws about debt collection. In fact, to go after him, I'd need to hire a collections attorney.

Oh — and although the judge said Montgomery was responsible for my credit card debt, the credit card companies didn't care. My name was on the card. They were not party to the divorce. I was supposed to pay up.

9. Get everything you need during the discovery phase of divorcing a sociopath

I was convinced that Montgomery had hidden money somewhere. He'd swindled women out of more than $1 million over eight or nine years — I couldn't imagine that it was all gone.

Looking over my divorce records, I discovered that we never received some of the bank records we'd subpoenaed — records that might show where his money was. I asked my lawyer to get the records. She wouldn't.

The period of time between filing the complaint for divorce and the actual trial is called the discovery phase. During this period of time, information, such as bank statements, correspondence and other records, can be subpoenaed. But once discovery closes, you can no longer subpoena records.

Therefore, it is very important to get every document you may need during discovery, because after the trial it is too late.

10. Judgment debtors can avoid payment by declaring bankruptcy

As I started searching for my money, I talked to a high-powered international collections attorney who gave me terrible news: All my ex-husband had to do to avoid paying me was to declare bankruptcy.

Court judgments can be discharged through bankruptcy — except in cases of fraud.

I had claimed in my divorce that my ex defrauded me. However, the divorce decree did not include a statement of fraud. Therefore, I had to go back into court to have my divorce decree modified to include the judge's findings of fraud. Which cost me more money.

I conducted an international search for Montgomery's money. But in the end, I found nothing. All I collected from him was $517. Still, because the court found him guilty of fraud, I am able to tell all of you exactly what happened.

By the way, after hearing the divorce horror stories of so many Lovefraud readers, I realize that my divorce was one of the easy ones. If you're divorcing a sociopath, you really need to know what you're up against. Lovefraud's webinars can help you. I recommend that you check them out.

Children with a sociopath:
Do you stay or do you go?

Finally figuring out, after years of marriage and a couple of kids, that your partner is a sociopath, is a good news/bad news situation.

The good news: You are not crazy. You were not imagining things and you were not overreacting. There is a bona fide, medical reason for the insanity you have been enduring — your spouse has a serious personality disorder.

The bad news: Now that you know what the problem is, you need to figure out what to do about it — and all of the options are difficult.

I'm writing this blog in response to the post in the Lovefraud Forum submitted by "Gccc," called *16 years, 2 children later, my life imploded. A death of sorts.* Following is what she wrote.

The Vortex of Hell

This is my first time reaching out to anyone. I believe this is how I will begin my healing process.

I had never been able to explain what I described as the "Vortex of Hell" I have been living in for many years. When he was caught, with no way out, of participation on sex/date websites, he denied it — with the concrete proof in my hands. Then I knew this is really more than my worst nightmare.

But it wasn't the betrayal of that. It was the absolute callous and arrogant response that killed me so much more. It was the years prior to that. I had never experienced a coldness that left me alone, desperate to confirm that he loved me somehow when he broke me into pieces at the moments I needed him to hold my heart the most. And it was, and still is, the desperation to find love or comfort from the one that hurt me the most in the first place.

The torture of that alone is astounding. I could not begin to explain what this is to most of my family. He LOVES me so much! He ADORES me! They have no clue that I believe that he actually despises everything about me. His words never match his actions.

Right now I am invested in a 14-year marriage with a 13- and 10-year-old who are the most beautiful, pure and honest things. How do I pull their world out from under them? And I don't want them to be exposed to him without my protection and diversion. I can sacrifice my life to keep that from them because I love them that much.

I have got to get myself help! I am not sure if this is what it is, but my life couldn't be explained any better than the patterns of crazy I've read about for months. It gives it a validity and it is real, concrete, and I'm not crazy, though I am after I deal with the sick cycle over and over. I need to connect to begin my journey.

4 facts about sociopaths and children

Usually, when you're involved with a sociopath (Lovefraud's definition of a sociopath is someone with antisocial, narcissistic, borderline, histrionic or psychopathic personality disorder) the standard advice is to leave and then go No Contact — never communicate with the person, in any way, ever again.

But when you have children with a sociopath, things get complicated. Here are facts about sociopaths, and what these facts mean for your situation.

1. Sociopaths do not love their children

Sociopaths are incapable of loving anyone, and that includes their children. Sometimes they can put on a good Mother or

Father of the Year act. But if you observe carefully, you'll see that they view the kids as property, servants, or mini-me's. They are more concerned with how the kids make them look than they are about their children's actual wellbeing. Gccc said she is willing to sacrifice her life to protect her children. A sociopath will never do that.

2. Sociopaths are terrible parents

Even if sociopaths manage to take care of their kids — like they would a pet or a favorite car — they still engage in emotional and psychological manipulation. This is actually the best you can hope for. Depending on how disordered the sociopathic parent is, children can also suffer from neglect, physical abuse, sexual abuse, and all the other shocking depravation you see in news reports.

3. Sociopaths want power and control

If you decide to split up, the sociopath may very well fight you for custody of the children — even if he or she has ignored them since they were born. Why? Because he or she does not want to relinquish property, and remember, the children are property. Plus, the sociopath does not want to lose control over you, and the best way to control you is through the children.

4. Courts usually believe children need both parents

If your custody battle goes to court, understand that judges, lawyers and other court professionals are just as clueless about sociopaths as you once were. Therefore, they don't understand fact #2 — sociopaths make terrible parents. After all, research seems to say children do better when both parents are in their lives. Unfortunately, such research usually doesn't consider cases in which a parent is disordered. So unless there is documented physical abuse, the court is unlikely to keep the kids away from your ex.

So should you stay or should you go? Let's see how these facts affect your decision.

Considerations: Leaving the sociopath

1. The split is unlikely to be amicable — it could turn into a long, expensive divorce and custody battle, burning through all your assets. Despite any lip service about "the best interest of the children," the sociopath's main objective is to win, and crush you in the process. He or she will not willingly uphold obligations.

2. The children will not receive good parenting when they're with the sociopath. They may experience neglect and abuse. Or, they may be allowed to do whatever they want. In fact, the sociopath may encourage alcohol or drug use, violence or promiscuity.

3. The sociopath will probably disparage you and try to drive a wedge between you and the children. Or, the sociopath may try to buy the children off by giving them whatever they want.

4. You won't be able to control what happens when the children are with the sociopath. However, when the kids are with you, you can provide them with a calm, stable environment, and show them authentic love and caring. Kids are smart. If they are not disordered themselves, they will know the difference.

Considerations: Staying with the sociopath

1. The sociopath's manipulative, deceitful and abusive behavior — **towards you and/or the kids** — **will continue or even get worse.** Your children will see that you are tolerating the behavior. They'll grow up thinking abusive behavior is normal.

2. At best, you'll be doing all of the parenting yourself. If you're lucky, the sociopath will ignore the family. If you're not lucky, the sociopath will actively undermine you, the routines you want to establish, and your efforts towards discipline.

3. The sociopath may still disparage you, right to your face, in front of the kids. Your partner will be modeling abusive behavior, and kids learn from what they see.

4. Even as you try to show the kids love and warmth, there will always be an undercurrent of fear, anxiety, and "walking on eggshells" in the home. It will not be a healthy environment. The longer you stay in the environment, the more it will wear you down. At some point, even if the home becomes unbearable, you may not have the strength to leave.

So Gccc, there are many difficult decisions that you'll need to think through carefully.

5 tips for dealing with a sociopath

Lovefraud's standard advice for interacting with a sociopath is not to interact at all, to implement a strict policy of No Contact. Unfortunately, this isn't always possible.

Perhaps you share children with a sociopathic ex-partner. Or perhaps you have a disordered boss or co-worker, and aren't yet able to find new employment. Or perhaps some member of your family is disordered. If you have no choice but to interact with a problem person, here are some tips that may help you.

1. Do not react emotionally

Sociopaths will often do or say unpleasant things just to provoke a reaction out of you. Do not take the bait.

Remember, all sociopaths really want is to win. If they get an emotional reaction out of you, they view it as a win. It feeds them — and you don't want to feed sociopaths.

It's okay to be upset by what they say or do — just don't let them see it. When you are away from them, go ahead and yell, scream or cry. In fact, it's important to do this. You want to get your outrage out of your system, so that you can calm down and maintain your cool the next time they try to get under your skin.

2. Do not try to make them understand how you feel

If you have a problem with a normal person, you might try to explain your perspective in a non-judgmental way, using "I statements." For example, "When you use that tone of voice with me I feel like I'm back in grade school."

For this technique to work, you need to be dealing with someone who has empathy. Sociopaths do not have empathy, so you could turn yourself into a pretzel trying to explain your feelings, and they will never get it.

Also, don't try to hurt them so that they'll know how you feel. They won't be hurt — but they might get angry and come up with another way to retaliate.

3. Do not try to appeal to what's right

Sociopaths know, on an intellectual level, the difference between right and wrong. They just have no emotional attachment to doing what is right, and no moral inhibitions against doing what is wrong.

Therefore, any effort to convince them to do the right thing, just because it's right —for you, the kids, the company, whatever — is a waste of your breath.

4. Keep information to yourself

Say as little as possible to the sociopath. Remember that anything you say can and will be used against you.

Be especially careful not to reveal anything about your plans to the sociopath — or anyone who might convey information to the sociopath. This may include your own kids, friends and family. Sociopaths are very good at pumping others for information, often feigning "concern" about you.

5. Anything the sociopath says could be a lie

All sociopaths lie. Therefore, you should not believe any statement that the sociopath has ever made unless you have independent verification.

Even if the sociopath provides proof, it could still be false. Sociopaths routinely forge and fabricate documentation, websites, email exchanges and text messages. They also get other people to lie for them, although those people may not realize they are lying.

When you're dealing with a sociopath, everything is suspect.

About the author

Donna Andersen is author of Lovefraud.com, a website that teaches people to recognize and recover from sociopaths. She is also author of *Red Flags of Love Fraud—10 signs you're dating a sociopath* and the *Red Flags of Love Fraud Workbook*.

Donna learned about sociopaths the hard way—by marrying one. She tells the whole outrageous story in her first book, *Love Fraud—How marriage to a sociopath fulfilled my spiritual plan*. The book was awarded five stars by the Midwest Book Review.

Donna founded Lovefraud Education and Recovery. The nonprofit offers online webinars to help professionals and the public spot, escape and recover from narcissists, antisocials, psychopaths and other manipulators. She is co-author of a scientific paper about therapy for victims of sociopaths, and has presented research to the Society for the Scientific Study of Psychopathy.

Donna has appeared on television shows including *Insight* in Australia, *ABC News 20/20, Who the Bleep Did I Marry?, My Life is a Lifetime Movie, Handsome Devils* and *The Ricki Lake Show*. She has been interviewed for multiple radio shows, print articles and web posts.

Donna graduated summa cum laude from the Syracuse University with degrees in magazine journalism and psychology. She was the original editor of Atlantic City Magazine, and then founded a boutique advertising agency, Donna Andersen Copywriting, in 1983. Her portfolio includes multimedia scriptwriting, freelance magazine articles, newsletters, web content and more.

Donna is happily remarried, proving that recovery from betrayal is possible.